The Inevitable You®
Live Life by Design

William Sumner

The Inevitable You Live Life By Design
by William Sumner
Printed in the United States of America.

ISBN: 978-0-9835694-1-1

ACKNOWLEDGEMENTS

When I sat down and really reflected on whose DNA and input is in this book, I discovered there were a number of people to acknowledge. In my earliest life, playing football in Beavercreek, OH—Larry West, Paul Martin, and Bevan Garwood taught me the true meaning of greatness not only on the athletic fields of life, but even more importantly, off the fields, where it really started. At the same time, a number of teachers were instrumental in my mind's development, too many to mention all by name. Of note, however, Mrs. Gordon and Mrs. Van Ausdal, my English teachers, were unbelievable in so many ways. They challenged me to grow, and I will forever be in their debt.

Off to West Point, I met and experienced many outstanding officers and instructors, and some not so outstanding. Sometimes you learn more from the "not outstanding" ones than you do the good ones. Some people are in your life to inspire you, and some people serve as a warning. Of particular note was LTC Aschentino—that in a pivotal three-day period in the summer of 1975 he fundamentally changed my life is undisputable. I hope he knows what a truly outstanding leader he was for me. My classmates, *Proud and Great '78*, then and now continue to inspire me. Many continue to serve and have risen to great ranks, and many continued their greatness in other endeavors. My hat's off to all of you. When I joined the real Army, the soldiers and non-commissioned officers who took a wet-nose officer under their wing are too numerous to mention, but this does not lessen the deep gratitude in my heart for each and every one of you. Germany and the Men of the Marne Division, and especially my last assignment with the Rangers, for all my officers and NCOs cadre of Camp Darby— ooh-ra! You all rock! Your dedication to the mission and your professionalism to this day has never been equaled anywhere in my life.

Moving into "civilian" life in 1984—what a motivating business laboratory did I find! MCI was truly the "Wild West," and reporting into Texas to work for Skip Knowles along with Jim Gillum, Dennis McCumbee, Chris Craven, and the whole management team, I was again, a "wet-nose" young business manager deeply out of his element and eager to learn. They took me under their wings, and I am deeply indebted to all of them. Deserving special attention here is George Tronsrue. As my classmate at West Point, we went off to Germany and came back to Ft. Benning together—he was instrumental in helping me into MCI, and he also helped form the next pivotal chapter of my life. Metropolitan Fiber Systems began life as Chicago Fiber Optics where I was the third employee, right behind George, working for Tony Pompliano. I cannot say enough about Tony. We joked, but it was oh so true—we experienced life there in "dog years." And truly, working for Tony was as hard as cramming seven years of work into one year, but he made sure we extracted seven years of experience, too. He was a great man, I loved his laugh and rough humor, and I miss him dearly. Shifting back to MCI, I was extremely fortunate to work with some true superstars: Dan McGuigan, Andy Barrie, our client John Sandberg, and again, just too many people to mention. Life in the telecom revolution was grand indeed!

My life shifted again with the decision to obtain my Masters in Social Work. Aurora University had some of the finest, deepest, most-caring, and most-compassionate professionals I ever experienced. While all the dedicated staff deserves accolades, I would single out Dr. Janet Yanos and

Dr. Sara Bonkowski as having a most profound impact on my professional development. I owe them a deep debt of gratitude. Dr. Bonkowski was, especially, the professor who guided my Master's thesis which was published in 1997, a somewhat uncommon distinguished event, and I owe Sally deeply for that.

When I moved to Denver, the second job I had was with the US West Cable Group, and I moved out to California to aid in the acquisition and transition of Continental Cablevision. Again, you cannot imagine my luck! I have won so many lotteries in my life, and this was another profound one. One of the finest leaders I ever served under, Trey Smith, led a group of professionals who were simply amazing. Marwan Fawaz, Cindy Chalfant, Jim Matusoff and more, were kind to an inexperienced "bell head." They ensured my success! "Thank you" does not even begin to cover it.

And once again, my life spun to a radically new chapter. Departing corporate life in 2001, to begin this chapter of my life, within three months, I ran into Tony Robbins and RRI. That relationship has been wildly beneficial for me as I experienced profound new technologies and viewpoints. Of special note, Shore Slocum, Gary King, Jill Blessing, Rob Shelton and so many more opened their hearts and minds to educate me in a new arena. I am grateful to each and every one. Their impact to the content in this book is deep.

So in the last ten years, several other people deserve special mention. Eric Remer, Jim Scott, Andrew Albarelle, Steve Goldman, and Pete Leavell were instrumental in their own ways to challenge me, resource me, and while I took care of them the best that I could, I am deeply moved by their complete and total contributions to this project. They know what they did; they may not know how much it meant to me. Words cannot describe it; I am again limited to a "thank you" which is inadequate.

On this book itself, Jill Blessing deserves special mention. As Jib-Jab's tag line is *"Brilliant,"* I could not say that enough for her contribution. She took my voice... and made it better! She wrote in my voice, thought like me and better! Her DNA is deep in this book. I cannot tell you how amazing she is. I am deeply in her debt.

While not here as long as some of the others, his incendiary brightness, intensity, and utter drive to help serve *The Inevitable You*® mission, Justin McNamara deserves a special mark of gratitude. Here's to many more years and clients!

Of HUGE note—I must thank all my clients! Your DNA is DEFINITELY here! You have taught me, tolerated me, laughed at me/with me, cried, been moved, moved me... and so, so many more complex interactions. To each and every one of you... deeply... I say to you: I am honored you shared your most Sacred You with me. Without you, this project would never have become real. Thank you all...

Of special note:

Walter Goodwin, my brother, what can I say? You know what you gave me. Without you, there is certainly not this version of me! Thank you!

Bob Olds, my best friend and confidant since 1974 when two hayseeds from Ohio went to see the big city—I need no other words for you!

Tim Taylor and Jim Nalepa, my D-3 mates—to this day, you still inspire and move me. Thanks for your friendship and support.

Dr Robert Blaich: twice-monthly lunches for almost 18 years have enriched me with your wisdom, kindness, depth, and grace. Thank you. I know this world so much better for having known you.

For my family:

My sister Judy, who has risked much for my success, no words can express what you mean to me, to the project, to every word in this system. Big Sis: thanks for your sacrifices for me and for *The Inevitable® Clients*....

For my mother and father, Janet Mae and Ralph Sumner, they gave their all to me growing up so that I had a chance to succeed. Their love, their values, and their decency as human beings, left a deep impression and high standards on me that to this day beats in my heart and in my being.

I cannot describe what my children have meant to me. They have given much time to my clients, client calls, deliverables, clients who needed me at night or weekends, such that sometimes I missed my kid events and special moments. All four have supported both me and my clients, and... moreover, they have inspired me to be a better man and father because of who they are. Keane, Bonnie, Isabella and Jack—thank you.

And last, and certainly not least—my wife Barbara has sacrificed more than any man could ask a woman in his quest for his purpose and his greatness. One example, so that you will *really* know her specialness... When I began my MSW in 1992, I went into the program with *zero* background or experience—I needed to study that first semester literally every spare moment to survive. Barbara drove me every Tuesday and Thursday night to class from 6:00 to 10:00 pm so that I had an extra hour to study on the drive out and back. She did that for every class that entire semester, and she would sit in the lobby and wait for me! That is indeed a special woman. She is my soul mate, my muse, and so much more. I wish everyone could know her love.

For all the others, for anyone I may have not mentioned—search this book, and you will find you find your impact here... and I thank you.

With a team like this behind me, for my whole life, I am empowered to be the *Greatest Version of Me!* Thank you. Thank you. Thank you *all*!

FOREWORD

"If you change the way you look at things, the things you look at will change." —*Wayne Dyer.*

"ALL humans have _____ potential. And I emphasize... it's ALL, capitalize it, double-underline it... ALL humans... have_____ potential."

When I ask this question in introducing my seminars, most people know what word fills in the blank. They shout out, "unlimited," "infinite," or "boundless." There is always one tiny problem, however. *They* are a human. Yet, they don't believe that *their* potential is unlimited. There is this hidden parenthesis at the end of THEIR sentence—*except for me*—they think to themselves.

But that can't be true, can it? Have you *ever* met a four year-old who believes they're limited? What happens to us? Where does the train go so horribly off the tracks?

If you've picked up this book, if you've come to this material, chances are you're here because you are a seeker of knowledge, you are looking for answers, you are in pain, or perhaps you're an overachiever. For *whatever* reason that brought you to the pages of this book, be prepared to truly recover your destiny, to remember your unlimited potential, and to unlock the inevitable *YOU* that has been at the mercy of other people's world view. The system you're about to uncover was created from a number of ancient wisdom systems and newer, technology-based sciences blended together to truly release "old you" programs, patterns, and perceptions. The "new you" can now discover a tools-based and experientially driven system that proves you have heights you may have never imagined.

What happens to most people is this—they go to school and are told, "Sit down, shut up, and look like all the other kids in your row. Color within the lines, and we will give you an 'A'."

In spite of this programming, do you remember who you are? Have you settled for a life that is less-than but is the best that you can do with the tools you have right now? Or, are you reaching for more?

Whatever your response—to be even reading this book, you are above average! Would you like more greatness in your life?

Conventional psychology, current success teaching, and even traditional mental health systems will teach you that who you are and what you have is a result of genetics, training, culture, and other intrinsic values of life. They will give you a personality type, categorize you, and possibly classify you as broken, as a victim having a syndrome or disorder. There is a staggering number of people in this culture on medications as a result of their supposedly bio-chemical brokenness. Obesity is now so rampant that 300 active and retired generals and admirals have spoken out that it's a threat to national security! The sad statistics can go on and on as we continue to perpetuate negative patterns.

This book is a challenge to the conventional system. Every person reading this book has past successes. It might have been a part in a high school play. Maybe you've mastered an instrument or a second language. Can you remember a time when you were determined to have something—

you thought about it, you focused on it, you obsessed about it, and you *knew* you had to have it? What happened in that space? Yes, you got it. Maybe not always perfectly and maybe not exactly when you wanted it, but if you never gave up, *you got it.*

Now as an adult in a life, you are busy doing the best you can with the tools and strategies you have. You understand potentiality only as a concept that *should* apply to you. Your belief system, your reality mechanisms, and the life you are actually leading has created a blind spot in your life, and you don't remember that inevitability applies to you. It works for everybody else, but not you. You will get bad luck. You will sabotage yourself. You will fall short. You are not obsessed about, focused on, and determined to have the thing you say you want at this stage in life.

Now if the preceding paragraphs don't apply to you, you're an overachiever and you're absolutely great at getting what you want. And on your very bad days, you're still above average. However, in reality, your challenge is the same. The speed you travel is not as important as the direction. But, how can you change it? What should you do? What you are going to discover is that all of these things are not about you, it is more about *how you have been taught to <u>do</u> you.*

As you begin this book, you will discover much of your life contains neural recipes for success and failure, and by the end of this book, you are going to change how *you look at life.* You are going to take a thorough inventory of your beliefs, neural recipes, strategies, action plans, and reality creation mechanisms. Some of them are going to be quite good; others will require a larger shift. Regardless, you will discover by the end of this book that the life you have today can be moved to the right for more potential, more outcome, more joy, more energy, more hope, more laughter, and more love than you ever thought possible...

A NOTE ABOUT <u>JOURNALING</u>
AND WRITING DOWN ANSWERS

At the end of every chapter, there are some great questions to answer. These will help you assimilate the material. It is essential to write down your answers because it makes this process real. *You see it for what it is.* Often, I write down client sentences for them so they can see what they said when I am in session with them. If you adopt this process, you will see your own "programs" far more clearly. You'll be able to *commit* to what you're saying and visually associate to your own words in black and white. Otherwise, it's just floating around in your thoughts, which does not create success. "Floating" thoughts are vague and unsubstantial. Writing down your answers is valuable and eye-opening.

Journaling allows you to see what is really going on. What is the flow, what is the truth, what is the program, what is hiding, what are you NOT writing, and so much more.

Write to your heart's content—scribble, and doodle, dog-ear the pages. Use different pens, highlight stuff, tape in pictures, jot down notes, or use "stickies." You can type up stuff and tape or staple it in. *Make this book work for you! This is <u>your</u> road-map.*

My own journal is, in essence, my best friend. Of all the places in life I communicate—my journal knows every crook and crevasse that is ME. You will learn to love to journal. Write down what is really going on as you read this book. It is the *Inevitable You*® showing up!

PART 1:

The "Old You"

WILLIAM SUMNER

CHAPTER ONE:
Your Future, Your Choice

*You are only a small reflection of
what is possible and inherent within you.*

There is a potential in you greater than *anything* you have ever imagined.

You are an unstoppable, magnificent force with the potential for deep fulfillment and infinite prosperity. You are perfection. *You are inevitable.*

Yet... if you are like most people, even if you are able to fully comprehend this statement, you still cannot fully embrace it. Somehow, we innately understand that human life is divine and powerful. But, when it's applied to our own life, there is a hidden parenthesis—(except me), (but not right now), or (maybe someday).

Can you even remember the last time you felt completely free and unbounded? Can you think of a time when you were uninhibited by rules, doubts, fears, and worries? The child version of you was not burdened in this way. The four-year-old version of you had no idea that he or she could not become or do absolutely anything in life. Our deepest self knows no boundaries and has no fears. Our truth always triumphs. Is there *any* four-year-old who doesn't learn to ride a bike?

So, what happens to us over the years? And, more importantly, how can we get back on track?

We all experience pain, misfortune, heartbreak, and disillusionment in life, and over time, we all create boundaries, stories, and layers to protect ourselves from the hard lessons we've learned through life. However, instead of taking those difficulties and using them to enrich our natural power, we often grow fearful, hide our true gifts, and reinforce our protective shields.

But, there is an alternative, more empowering, and more authentic approach. You have the power to choose a better future and to leave your past behind.

In fact, once you finish reading this book, you'll understand—you have *both* the divine perfection with which you were born *and* the skill and experience that only comes through life's trials and errors.

It is up to you to decide how to use those tools to enrich your future.

The Inevitable You® Process

The fact that you bought this book is a good sign. It indicates you are looking for a shift at some level. Whether you are coming from a great place, an above average place, a place of pain, a place of resignation, or a place of compromise, there are two parts of you. One part is in top form—it functions well, and it has gotten you everything that you consider good and successful so far in life. In contrast, the other part of you is laden with challenges and obstacles. It's the part of you that you don't like. It's the part you would desperately like to change if you could.

This book addresses *both* parts. You are about to uncover the best in you, *and* you are going to make it *even better*. You are also going to deeply examine the challenged part of you. However we aren't going to just work on fixing or enhancing it; we're going to permanently and forever remove it from the reality of who you think you are.

I developed *The Inevitable You*® system a number of years ago. I was in the presence of a great mentor and friend of mine, and during the course of our conversation, he said to me: "Imagine a circle of light in front of you and move towards it. When you step into that light, who you are, what you're going to become, is inevitable. *You* are inevitable."

This concept clicked with me. I got it. I said "Yeah, that's who I am. I am a part of that unbounded light. I know why I'm here." And, there's a reason why you are here, as well.

The Inevitable You® is designed to take the best of the best in personal growth, psychology, and leadership, to mold it into a framework you can access, and to translate it so that you can apply it to your own life. It's designed to help you discover and embrace who you are, and why you came here to be.

Finding Your Trajectory

But, what does it really mean to be inevitable?

It's about finding your path, it's about living up to your full potential, and it's about stepping into a trajectory towards your destiny. I've chosen the word, "trajectory," very carefully.

Stepping into *The Inevitable You*® is not a winding journey full of pit-stops, and segues. Rather, a trajectory is a driven force. It's about acceleration and rising momentum. It's similar to a journey in that it implies you are on a path, however, it's also much more. Being on a trajectory is about moving with direction, purpose, and confidence. It's about moving steadfastly with total focus so that your final destination, no matter the exact course chosen, is inevitable.

Do you know where your current trajectory is heading?

What has been the direction of *your* life thus far? What has happened in your past? What is your personal history. What brought you to this place. How did you come across this book?

The fact is—there are a certain number of doors you have been both consciously and unconsciously creating for yourself over time. There are decisions you have embraced, possibilities you've ignored, and opportunities you haven't even noticed. And, you will continue to do so over time (whether you realize it or not).

So, do you know where you are currently heading? Do you know which doors you are entering, which you are avoiding, and which you are blindly passing by?

There are three keys to finding out.

First, you must fully believe that *all results begin with a thought.* You may have heard this before, and you may agree on some level, but you may have a few exceptions to the rule. Perhaps it's easy to see the connection between thought and result in some areas of your life. However, when events in your life become challenging, it's not as easy to see the link, or perhaps it's simply hard to make the connection on a large scale.

For example, you may not be able to grasp the notion (yet) that one little thought can trigger a tsunami or a stock market crash.

The second key to understanding your trajectory is to fully acknowledge that *emotions catalyze the power of your thoughts.* Emotions are the juice, the electricity, and the lighter fluid of life. When you're in an intense emotional state, your hypothalamus floods your body with neural peptides that communicate directly to your physical body. Thus, when you're intensely happy, all the cells in your body are also happy, which benefits your entire body—your cells expand and allow a positive inner and outer flow. Likewise, when you're angry, all the cells in your body are also angry. In fact, they contract and become restrictive the angrier you get. Thus, managing your emotions will continually affect your trajectory (and your overall health) in life for better or worse.

Third, your current trajectory inherently relies on your acceptance and deep understanding that _all_ humans have unlimited potential, _including you_. You must understand this as a *fact*. Take a moment and really feel this sentence because here's the truth—you may be able to accept this on a philosophical level, however, when it really comes to fully owning this truth and employing its sheer magnitude in your own life, you likely fall short. You may be able to accept that human beings are unlimited; you may be able to see brilliance and talent in others; and you may even be able to philosophically try on this concept in your own life. However, all that is not enough—you must "get" this message on a very deep level.

You are a human, therefore you have unlimited potential.

It's that simple. Over the years, you may have been taught that you have limitations. You may have inaccurately deduced that your past struggles mean you are imperfect in some way. You may be struggling with deep-seated fears about the possibility of failure. However, take a moment now and read this sentence twice if you need to.

It's not your potential that's limited, it's the strategies you're using that need help.

It's your recipes that need to be updated, _not you_. The cookbook that you've been baking with all of your life was most likely passed on from parents who inherited those recipes from your grandparents, and in all likelihood, you've probably passed the same recipes on to your own children, as well.

You are operating with strategies that stem from an old consciousness. How you show up today is really an older version of you. When you were born, your family of origin gave you a blueprint for your life. They said, "This is who you are," "This is what you're good at," "This is what you're not good at," "This is what is good in life," and "This is what is bad about life."

And, even if you had a great coach or a great teacher who inspired you over the years to modify your blueprint, you're still only operating off of a slightly modified blueprint based on your old consciousness and unsupportive patterns. In order to truly change your current trajectory, you have to make a deeper mental shift.

Change Your Strategies, Not <u>You</u>

Think about this. Suppose you were born in a house trailer. However, as you grew in life, you moved into a better neighborhood and a better house. In fact, by now, you may even be living in a mansion or your own version of the Taj Mahal. Your difficult, awkward, or poor past is long gone, but in spite of your current conditions, you are *still* lugging that old house trailer along with you. And, it's not just the memory of the trailer that hinders you—it's the beliefs surrounding it, the people it represents, the painful baggage loaded inside, and the cumulative experience of all those things combined. No matter how far you've come in life and no matter how far in your past that trailer seems, *somehow* it's still always there. Someone may even come into your new home and says, "Wow what a great house you live in," and you'll think to yourself, "Yeah, but he doesn't know about the old, rusty trailer sitting in my back yard."

It's like one of those master combination locks from your old gym locker at school. Suppose your parents and your grandparents taught you that the combination to a fulfilling life is 12-18-12, and as a result, you have been working hard ever since to reach success by following that code. But, suppose the code isn't working. Have you tried a *different* code? Or, are you only pushing harder, working more intensely, and trying with all your might to no avail? Perhaps 12-18-12 was a combination that worked for your parents or grandparents, but that doesn't mean it's *your* code.

You're not stupid. You're not hopeless. You've just been using old psychology and old recipes for growth. Old thinking has likely helped you get to where you are, but it won't get you to the next level. You need to change, you need to transform, and you need to move forward. It's time to *elevate* your game.

This Program is Unlike Any Other

We are going to take a pretty big chunk out of your old consciousness and old patterns throughout this book. As a result, you will not only define your history, but you will *decide* what it means. You will re-evaluate who you think you are today, who you believe you could be, and what you think you're capable of accomplishing. I am going to give you the tools and awareness you need to understand a new reality, and I'm not just talking about a "motivational," mumbo-jumbo new reality either. This is not another "feel-good" book. In fact, if you understand and apply what I am about to share, I promise—*you will change.*

I'm not your traditional self-help guru. I am a successful businessman with a military background, and a deep part of my nature stems from the years I spent in the military and training at West Point. On the battlefield, there is no time for wavering or indecisiveness. When you have guns firing at you and lives at stake, you *must* focus solely on your mission. There is no other option. If you get off track, people *die*.

For better or worse, this critical mindset is now embedded in my DNA. It is something I apply to everything I undertake.

I am here to help *you* get *your* results, and I am just as committed and focused on this objective as if I were pulling you out of a war zone.

"Mission first. Mission always."

So, get ready to really make some changes. My system is about *results.* I've been called a motivational speaker before, and I don't really like those words because motivation is relative—it's not what truly drives us. We are all motivated to do what we want and to avoid that which we think will bring us pain. Do you have to dig very deep to find the motivation to enjoy a fully paid trip around the world? Are you be able to motivate yourself to accept a $100 million lottery prize? You don't need *motivation* from me. You're already motivated... about what you want.

Instead, this book will give you a new sense of awareness of about how a new reality can be. It's also going to give you the tools you need to get there. It's about how your brain functions and how *you create your reality*.

But, be advised—some of the strategies I use may be counterintuitive. They may challenge you to see things a little differently.

There is No Such Thing as "Weak Link"

For example, you've likely been laboring under a common misconception. Most educational and training systems teach under the "weak link" theory. Throughout life, you've probably learned that "fixing you" is the way to get better. However, my diverse background as a professional warrior, corporate salesperson, and operational executive in telecommunications has proven to me that trying to "fix you" is actually the worst way to improve. In fact, it's the least efficient path towards success.

We're not chains. We're not weak links. We're not machines. You cannot tap into your potential by fixing weaknesses. Take a moment to really ponder and feel this sentence:

"You don't tap into potential by fixing weaknesses."

If you've ever gotten your one-hour review at work, you likely went in and received a full three minutes of praise for all that you had done right in the previous quarter. Then, if your company is like most, your manager or boss spent the next 57 minutes completely dissecting your two most recent mistakes. *Why do managers always focus on the negative?*

Managers aren't necessarily bad people—they tend to focus on your mistakes or inadequacies because they believe that's the best way to get better results from you in the future.

But, their efforts are misguided. Fixing your weaknesses can actually only *slightly* improve your performance, and there are far better ways to create a better you. Enhancing your strengths and adding to your existing greatness is what really creates movement and momentum in life.

It's About YOU, Not Me

Another challenge in the self-help, personal growth industry is a lot of the speakers and teachers (although they are wonderful men and women) tend to teach about the way *their* world is. They don't necessarily get into *your* world. I've been very conscious to make this coaching system about *you,* and I want to make sure you make it about you, too. We both don't need another Bill Sumner; we both want a greater you.

Traditional Psychology is Old

Finally, traditional psychology and traditional self-help are simply *old*. They're based on such things as Freudian principles that were relevant 120 years ago, however, there are new, better tools available today. There have been scientific breakthroughs in neurology since then that can massively affect your reality.

Think of it this way. Just a hundred years ago, there were still several well-intended doctors and nurses who thought putting leaches on fingers to suck out evil vapors was a useful healing remedy, even though anti-bacterial soap had been around for decades. Similarly, there are traditional psychologists and teachers practicing *old* models today when new, more advanced remedies exist.

This system utilizes some of the great foundational elements found in old models. However, it also incorporates ancient wisdom systems and some of the latest breakthroughs available from science-based technologies. I've endeavored to combine the best of the best in a comprehensive system for you.

The Work is Up to You

However, all of the knowledge in the world cannot help you shift if you're not committed to some hard work. You're going to have to play a part in your transformation to make all of this last.

Change is not a process; change is an *event*. It's important that you not only take the time to ponder the questions at the end of each chapter, but that you actually write down and commit to your responses. I'll be here to help you.

Think of me as your mental trainer.

I'm not only going to present you with a new consciousness, I'm going to help you enhance, create, maintain, and grow that new consciousness. I'm introducing you to new tools and helping you build new muscles so that you can create a "new you." Just as a personal trainer takes you into the gym to help you build new muscles by teaching you new exercises, I'm going to take you into a *mental* gym. I'm going to teach you how to stretch parts of yourself you didn't even know existed, and I'm going to share some tools that will challenge you to consistently build both your mental and emotional muscles. By the time you finish reading, you will have created a new and more elevated blueprint for your life.

Keep Your Mind Open

And, in order to help me help you, I ask that you challenge me. Test me. Test what you're about to read. Test the information. But, test it to find *value* for yourself, not as a means to keep yourself stuck in a place that you don't want to be. Make sure it passes your own smell test, but don't dismiss it just because it's unfamiliar. You may have to really think about some of the things I'm about to share. So, challenge what doesn't resonate with you from a learning perspective. Consider what value it *might* have for you if you embraced the concept. Keep your mind open and read actively.

So, let's get started.

Defining Your Blueprint

You've likely heard the question: "Is your glass half full or half empty?" Some of you have a full glass, some of you have an empty one, and some of you believe you should fake a full glass regardless of how you really feel. Well, here's what's trippy—*none* of these approaches work because the *glass is always* both *full and empty.*

The question is never about the glass; it's always about *you.* How you see the glass is how you see the world. It's a reflection of the mental software you're currently running, but it's not who you really are. If we took a snapshot of you today and looked at your hairstyle, the clothes you're wearing, and your environment, we're not really looking at you—we're looking at what you think, feel, and believe at this point in time. We're looking at how you currently process the world. However, if you decide to update your current software, you will instantly evolve.

Whatever reason that brought to you the pages of this book, be prepared to truly recover your destiny, to remember again your unlimited potential, and to unlock *The Inevitable You*® that up until this point has been at the mercy of other people's views of the world.

Before moving on to the next chapter, take some time to really think and write out your answers to the following questions. Write out your answers, be real with yourself, be impeccably honest, and have fun with your responses. I promise—if you take the time to write this out and apply the principles (to be revealed throughout this book) behind each question, *you will see a shift.*

- Who are you right now? (Be as specific as possible—this is your current mental snapshot and it's a vital part of "The Inevitable You®" system.)

- What is your world view?

- Complete these sentences: I am…, Strangers are…, The world is….

- What do you want to get out of this book? Do you want a better relationship? A better job? A better career? Do you want to be a better parent? Do you want better health? What do you <u>really</u> want?

- If I gave you all the money, all the time, and all the resources to create your life, what are your dreams? What are your visions? What do you really want for yourself?

- On a scale of 1 to 10, (10 being highest), rate yourself on how powerful, magical, and extraordinary you think you are?

CHAPTER TWO:
The Seven Myths

*Find the one corrupted, mental software code
that when healed, will cause the whole program
to run as it's designed.*

First things first.

Did you answer the questions from the last chapter?

Remember, this book is a process. I've worked with thousands of people, and trust me—in order to actually experience a shift, you have to put in the effort! Your answers reflect your current mental blueprint and your way of experiencing the world.

It is a snapshot that represents what you currently focus on, what you believe in, what you value in life, where you want to go, and your rules to get there. Unconsciously, it is the master plan of your life. In fact, each day (whether you realize it or not), you are continually building upon and making decisions based on this plan.

And, now that you have that snapshot, I want to spend some time looking more closely at the part of you that you'd like to change. It's time to examine the "old you."

For some this makes sense. You want to progress. You want to make a quantum leap into your future. You are more than ready to release the "old you."

However, for some of you, letting go of the "old you" is a scary idea. The "old you" can be like a comfortable pair of shoes. You know they are falling apart and in disrepair, but it doesn't seem like anything else will ever feel as safe and familiar. If this is true for you, you may be simply enjoying the *contemplation* of taking a quantum leap. And, that's okay. You don't need to leap right now.

Your Beliefs

Your beliefs are a key place to start. At your core, they drive your purpose and your life choices. They can be global (what you believe about the world) and personal (how you see yourself). Some beliefs will bring out the best in you, whereas others hold you back. Here are a few examples of globally empowering beliefs: "People are basically good," "Life balances itself out," "The world can be a great place," "When someone works really hard, they are often rewarded."

In contrast, globally disempowering beliefs might be: "People are always out to cheat me," "Life is not fair," "Sometimes good people just have bad luck."

Personal empowering beliefs might be: "I can do anything I set my mind to," "There is always a way to solve a problem (and _another_ one)," and "I am full of possibilities."

And, personal disempowering beliefs might be: "I eventually drive away people who love me," "Every time I try to succeed, I manage not to succeed," and "I can't get ahead."

Beliefs are prevalent in our everyday thinking, and they are broadcast by the media, within families, and through our peer groups. They are literally *everywhere*, and unfortunately, the disempowering ones hold on like stubborn leeches on our brains.

The following are seven common beliefs that have been perpetuated by Hollywood, society, your school system, and your family. Virtually everyone believes these myths to be true. They are stories that you have likely considered true for most (if not all) of your life, and they are mostly unconscious.

Myth 1: You are Broken

There is a notion that who you are today, and why you are who you are, is stagnant or unchanging. People will tell you, "Oh, it's okay who you are. It's not your fault. That trauma happened to you—you were a victim. It's okay that you're broken now. I feel sorry for you."

And, if you're broken more than a little, your psychiatrist will tell you, "No worries—we have a great pill for you. It'll help modify your behaviors, and you'll feel better."

Now, the fact that the pill may not actually *heal* you is immaterial—you are broken, so your psychiatrist is happy to give you a pill to make you feel better.

Please don't get me wrong. By making these types of statements, I am not disparaging health professionals. The last doctor to put a leech on somebody's finger to suck out evil vapors did so with a pure heart and a great intention to heal, and I'm sure the psychiatrists prescribing drugs today do so with an equally pure heart.

That said, this is key—most (if not all) of that diagnosis stuff is garbage! *You're not broken.* There's nothing wrong with *you*; there are only things wrong with your program, your strategies, and your patterns. You wouldn't look at a corrupted piece of software and go, "Oh, the computer's bad—let's throw it away." You would just reload the software, or you would upload a new program. Same goes for your mental blueprint.

I know it's hard to remember this simple principle when you're in the depths of life. It's counterintuitive. When the storm surge is high and garbage is flying through your life, it's easy to fall back on more primitive forms of programming and old defense systems.

But, this tendency is also linked to those family-of-origin programs I described in the last chapter. Your old patterns have been passed down unconsciously through generations. I'm not saying your parents and grandparents weren't amazing people. When I make this statement, people will say, "But Bill, my parents gave me great messages about me and look who I have become."

But, that's not what I'm saying. You must understand—your programming doesn't necessarily come from what your ancestors thought about and *told you.* Unfortunately, the imbedded lessons you've ingrained over time came from something even more powerful. They stem from what your ancestors believed about *themselves.* In every generation, every person in your family did the best he or she could with the resources at his or her disposal, but at a core level, you will only believe in yourself as much as your parents believed in themselves. Does that make sense?

One of the biggest challenges I experience with people I work with is a notion that somehow, because of a trauma or some other unsolvable past challenge, their life is now forever messed up. I hear things like, "I lost all my money," "I was bankrupt," "I was molested," "I was raped," "I was criminalized," "I had alcoholic parents," etc... But, as horrible as all of those experiences are, and as much as I feel for you, your past is in the past. You can't change it. It did happen, but who you are today is *not* fixed and rigid. You can create a "new you."

One of the reasons why traditional psychology and therapy is upsetting to me is because 90 percent of the profession reinforces the opposite. A central part of therapy relies on analyzing the past. They'll say, "Well, you were traumatized, so your problem today is not your fault. Let's take the adult you back and visit the little you. See there you are—it's your parent's fault; it's the criminal's fault; it's the circumstances that traumatized you—it's not your fault. I love you. (Noogie!) You're okay despite being broken."

Myth 2: You're Going to Have a Limp

Think about this for a moment: What if you left home today like any other day and got into a terrible accident on your way to work. Due to this accident, suppose you severely break your thigh bone in the crash, and it's an ugly, traumatic break—the bone is sticking out, and there's dirt in the wound. It's terrible. Then, when you get to the hospital, the emergency staff says to you, "Hey, great news, one of our greatest orthopedic surgeons is on staff today and he is going to take a look at you."

You are thrilled to be under such great care, right? When the surgeon comes in, you completely trust his professional diagnosis. He looks at your leg and says, "Okay, the good news is I can fix this. It's really, really bad. It's one of the worst breaks I've seen, but I can fix this. The better news is—you're going to walk, and that's great. But, the bad news is—you're going to walk with a limp. 90 percent of my patients like you end up walking with a limp. I don't want you to get your hopes up about healing completely."

And so, you accept your fate, complete rehab, and walk with a limp for the rest of your life.

Now, in a parallel universe, let's say the exact same scenario happens simultaneously. You experience a terrible leg break, the bone sticks out and you go to the emergency room. They say, "One of our best orthopedic surgeons is on staff." He comes in, he looks at you, but this time, he says, "Hey, good news—I can fix this, the even better news is you're going to be able to walk, and the greatest news is you're going to walk perfectly fine. It's going to take rehab, and I'm not going to kid you, rehab is going to be hard, but you're going to walk fine. 90 percent of my patients who experience traumatic breaks such as this are able to fully recover. You're going to walk fine."

And, so you do.

Now, here's the moral of both stories: *Your body will do what your mind believes is possible.* The 10 percent of people who walked perfectly even after the first doctor told them they would not, did so because they told themselves, "Screw that, I'm not going to limp." So, they figured out a way in spite of their small-minded doctor (who afterwards proclaimed, "It's a miracle!").

And, the 10 percent of people who didn't recover even though the second doctor told them they would took the worst action possible. They did nothing. Healing is a dynamic process that we don't fully understand, but you have to do your part to progress—physically and mentally.

And, here's another tidbit. Understanding how you can heal yourself gets even trippier when you factor in the innate wisdom of your body. When your body heals itself, it doesn't just look at your leg break and go, "Well gee, I had a weak spot in the bone, I'm just going to put enough calcium back there to make the leg bone whole again." It goes, "Holy smokes! I had a break here. I've got to put in more calcium, more healing matrix, and I've got to boost my immune system. We've got to really build this bone up so this doesn't happen again!"

In fact, the very spot in the bone that is broken will not only repair itself, it will become the strongest part of that bone. Eventually, a broken leg will be even stronger than the other good leg. Therefore, after your "terrible accident," not only are you are not a limper, you are actually even more powerful than you were before.

Can you see how this story might apply to other parts of your life, as well?

Think about this. Have you ever experienced an emotional or mental trauma that inspired somebody to say to you, "Hey, the good news is you're going to be okay, but the bad news is you're going to be depressed, sad, anxious, unfulfilled, or dependent on someone else from now on."

As a result of this prediction, perhaps you've consequently been "limping" for the past 20 or 30 years.

Well, I have some news for you—the very thing that broke your heart, the very thing that traumatized you—it's now the *strongest* part of you. You just have to know how to frame it that way to yourself from now on, you have to *choose* to experience it that way, and you have to put in the effort required.

You can make this shift instantaneously. If you so choose, you can heal your mind in the time it takes to upload a new software program on your computer. And, how long does it take to upload software? Just a few minutes, right?

Instead of allowing yourself to feel weak, tell yourself, "I now have a powerful heart. I have a powerful, magical psychology. I am an incredible being because this trauma has made me that much stronger, that much greater."

This will turn your life around.

Don't get me wrong. I realize it can be very difficult to approach trauma. Sometimes it's hard to go there, but the problem for most people is that they don't look for the *strength* in trauma. They only look at the pain.

However, when you begin to ask yourself a different set of questions such as, "How did this trauma benefit me," or "What is the true strength that I have," you will be able to overcome literally anything placed in your path, regardless of what your doctor (or anyone else) tells you.

Positive thinking does work. In fact, you may have even already applied it to some aspects of your life. But, will you be able to stay strong even if someone tells you, "You're a child of divorce," "You're a child of alcoholic parents," "You have a gene defect," or "You have a disorder."

What if a trusted professional is convinced you will need to be medicated for life? What will you do? You definitely don't want to be on meds, but you don't want to have a horrible problem either, and there may not seem to be any other strategy available.

Don't worry. That's what this book is for. I'm here to give you alternative options to transform your past traumas or negative experiences into new strengths. You can use the power of your mind to transform your potential. You have the capacity to become even stronger in spite of something terrible.

You're not broken.

You're not a limper.

You are already even stronger than before you started this chapter.

The desire to take your trauma and turn it into joy and goodness is already embedded in your DNA. It's just you haven't known how to access it. Once you finish reading this book, you're going to celebrate your traumas and newfound strengths.

But, along the way, remember this...

Myth 3: Change is a Process

This myth is persistent. I often ask the audience during my seminars, "Raise your hand if you think change is a process," and virtually everyone will raise his or her hand. But, really think about this—is change actually a process? It's not. Change actually happens instantaneously *in the very moment* you make a decision to transform.

Traditional psychology often counters this notion. You may have heard a psychologist say, "There's a process for change, and if you work really hard, you're going to be able to make a shift."

But, I say, "No."

All the work actually lies in the *process leading up to the change."*

When you study how the mind works, there is literally a single instant when you stop doing what you don't want to do and start doing what you want to do. It sounds simple, but once you understand this concept, you can figure out how to change at any level *immediately.*

And, why would you want to waste your time processing stuff to get to the place where you really want to be? Just go there!

Maybe you're afraid. That's normal. People often say things like, "Change is scary," or "I'm really afraid to change." And, to the extent that you're scared, you are. You can't change that, but what is really driving the fear? Are you really afraid of the change itself, or is it what you think the change will or won't bring you that's nerve-wracking?

There is an alternative. Start practicing the ability to change your thinking in the moment. Ask yourself, "What am I sick of in my life? What will I no longer tolerate?" Then change it right away and move on.

Here's another common myth.

Myth 4: Incremental Change is Better

Several systems will tell you, "Don't go cold turkey, don't go massive. Take baby steps."

However, there are several reasons to think otherwise. In the early 2000s, there was a great study cited in the e-zine, *Fast Times.* The article was entitled, "Change or Die," and it posed this question: "If a trusted medical authority told you that you would die unless you made a radical shift in at least one of three areas, such as diet, exercise, or stress, would you make the change?"

Remarkably, over 90 percent of those studied would rather die than change. (The participants were coronary bypass patients.)

However, there was one doctor whose results went against the norm. Rather than accepting death over change, his patients had an almost eight-fold improvement rate! A staggering 77 percent of his patients successfully changed their lifestyle even though their peers failed. So, what was he doing differently? Only one thing. Instead of asking his patients to change in increments, he taught them to make massive, radical actions to transform their lives.

So, why did his approach work? Let me use a different analogy to make it a little easier to understand. I call this my "15 Twinkie Theory."

Let's say you've been eating 15 Twinkies every day for as long as you can remember, but one day, your doctor tells you, "If you don't cut back on Twinkies, you are going to die. Every week, I want to you cut a Twinkie out of your diet until they are no longer a problem."

Now, let's go deeper into the mind of an individual who's faced with death, threatened by their mortality, and forced to eat *only* 14 Twinkies instead of 15. The irony is they don't even really think about the joy of eating 14 *entire* Twinkies. Instead, these sugar addicts obsess about the *one Twinkie* they didn't get. They'll think to themselves, "Oh, my God, this is *so* hard. This is *really* tough. How am I going to make it through this diet? Life is so hard when I don't get to eat 15 Twinkies."

Then, during the second week when the patients have to cut out two Twinkies, it's not just twice as difficult for them—it's five times as difficult! They'll say, "Oh, my Gosh! Two Twinkies gone? This is insanity. This is driving me crazy. This is *so* hard."

By week three, when they must cut out three Twinkies, it's absolutely the *end of the world* for these people!

Worse, when they get on a scale to see the results from all their "hard work," what do you think they see? Negligible results, obviously. They've only cut out a few Twinkies each day, which is not enough to make a difference.

When push comes to shove, baby steps will only give you baby results. However, the mounting psychological damage and stress behind an "incremental" diet will drive you crazy. If you are like 90 percent of the population on this type of diet, as soon as you have the opportunity, you will conclude the diet isn't worth it and start wolfing down Twinkies like there's no tomorrow.

The consequential aftermath of this decisions will further your downward spiral. You'll binge at a party or late at night by yourself and wake up the next morning feeling terrible. You'll say to yourself, "You know what? I can't do this. It's too hard. If I'm going to die, I might as well die fat and happy." And with that, you go back to eating 15 Twinkies a day.

Ever been there?

This is why over 90 percent of those faced with death versus changing their daily habits would rather just stick with their addiction than prolong life.

So now, let's look at what Dr. Ornish, the doctor whose patients had a 77 percent success rate, did differently. Instead of having his patients cut out Twinkies in increments, Dr. Ornish told them they could not have *any* Twinkies, effective *immediately*.

Interestingly, the psychological challenge of cutting out all 15 Twinkies actually created the same level of anxiety as only cutting out one.

And, by week two, it was equally hard for Dr. Ornish's patients to not eat Twinkies. However, there are two critical variables that made their experience much more effective than their peers.

First, when they got on the scale to see the results of all of their hard work, they saw massive results right away and felt really good about it. Second, when they fell back and occasionally gave in to their Twinkie temptation, they did not need as much sugar to enjoy the experience. Eating only one Twinkie was sufficient.

In fact, for Ornish's patients, eating any more than two or three Twinkies didn't even *taste* good. When your body is clean from sugar for three weeks, a little bit of sugar will taste great, but having more will not be enjoyable.

When traditional psychology tells you to "take baby steps" in order to change, it is setting you up to fail. I know this is counterintuitive. You've been told your whole life that quitting cold turkey is really hard, but I'm here to tell you—it's not.

By the fourth week on Dr. Ornish's diet, his patients were completely Twinkie-free. And, as their weight continued to come down, they started to settle into a normal life. If they occasionally craved a Twinkie, they had one. No big deal.

So, for whatever you are trying to change in your life, don't just take baby steps, okay? Go for massive, radical change. Incremental change literally will kill you.

The next myth is a covert operator. This myth works under cover. Here's how...

Myth 5: "The Rogue Program"

Many people are actually unconsciously working against themselves. If you say you want to make a change, is that *really* what you want at your core? Does the fat person want to be thin? Does the depressed person *really* want to be happy? Does the angry person *really* want to be calm? On a conscious level, of course you want to change. However, there is also a deeper, more insidious truth working against you. I call it "The Rogue Program" or "The Villain Program."

Here's how it works. Let's say you really want to lose weight, you hate your body, and you've been working to lose weight for years. Although you have been working hard to change by exerting energy focusing on the *fat you want to lose*, you are actually creating a program in your brain that will trigger you to gain *even more* weight.

I know this is counterintuitive, but if you change your thinking from "I hate fat; I don't want to be fat," to "I love thin; I want to be thin and powerful," you will improve your end results.

Allow me to go even deeper. If you've been trying to lose weight for a long time, you probably have a story about why you haven't had any success.

If this is true for you, I'm going to argue that at a deeper level, you don't really want to be thin, and here's why.

I know nobody wakes up in the morning and says, "Hey, I've got a great plan for myself! I'm going to eat 15 Twinkies and put on two more pounds today. That's a path of happiness for me."

Instead, most people who want to lose weight get up, look at themselves in the mirror, feel disgusted with their weight and with their body. They literally hate themselves for what they have become. Unfortunately, this type of emotion and energy creates a lot of deep, unconscious programming, and it's not worth the long-term damage (not to mention personal suffering). Self-loathing won't actually *do anything* to help the situation. You have to look deeper to understand what's at the root.

Here's what really happens...

First, your friend tells you about a new diet. Your friend tells you he or she has lost weight using this new program, and you say, "Wow! I think I'll try that." So, you get online, you do some research, go the grocery store, and buy some new food. Within a few weeks, it works! You start losing weight, and people start to notice. However, once people start recognizing the change in you, a very curious thing happens.

You're looking *so* great that your belief system starts to kick in, and suddenly there are no more excuses for the other parts of your life that aren't up to par. Your beliefs tell you, "Time to be amazing. Update your résumé. Dump that relationship. You need to start making some changes to live up to this new persona."

But then, your ego chimes in and tells you, "Wait a second. I know you— you're not amazing. You're still not good enough. You still don't deserve all these things. This "new you" is an illusion. You're about to destroy yourself!"

Now, the ego isn't trying to sabotage you, it's telling you these things out of love (albeit a mistaken love). It just wants to protect you from any potential future pain.

However, regardless of its intentions, once the ego chimes in, its damage is done. In that space, in that *moment* when your unconscious battles with your ego, if you let your guard down—*that's* when you give into the cravings around you. You tell yourself, "Who could follow that diet anyway? This diet doesn't work for me," and consequently you'll then proceed to indulge in an entire tub of ice cream.

Do you see the truth in this situation? Can you see how your true fear has nothing to do with weight?

You have more pain associated with what being thin really means you'll have to become. That hidden seed is the rogue, the villain, and it's why you really don't want to be thin... *yet*.

By the way, I'm using weight as a metaphor to explain this hidden program, however, it applies to all aspects of life.

For the depressed person, your rogue program will tell you that the consequences attached to being happy are potentially more painful than being depressed and upset. For the angry person, your rogue program will tell you that anger is jet fuel for motivation and energy.

Whatever it is you may want that seems to be out of your reach, you just have to find the hidden program stopping you (although you may have to dig to get there). I'll share more on this later.

Next...

Myth 6: "Don't spill the milk!"

I've saved the best two myths for last. Myth number six is one of the most persistent ways the "old you" nags. It's not that you are dumb, lacking talent, or unlucky. You have literally been *wired* to fail while attempting to command success!

Let me give you an example of what I mean.

Can you remember back to a time when your mother may have said something to you like, "Hey little Billy, don't spill the milk. Be careful, and don't spill the milk."

Two really bad things happened to you in that moment. First, in order to even comprehend that command, you had to think about every possible way you *could spill* the milk to avoid doing so. In fact, in order to please your parents, you probably went through 50 or so different ways you *might* spill the milk so you could figure out how to cognitively negate them.

If you did a PET scan on little Billy's brain after receiving this command, the part of his brain linked to "spilling milk" would be completely lit up. By trying to avoid it, his entire focus is on what he *doesn't want*.

This is another counterintuitive area of life. The harder you try *not* to spill the milk, the more ways you will think of to do <u>just that</u>.

Interesting, huh?

But unfortunately, that's not the worst thing that happens during this process. While you're busy focusing on *not spilling milk*, the emotions you feel at that moment are triggered, creating a lasting imprint on your psyche. Once stimulated, your brain will start to translate what the entire experience *means* to you. It will evaluate the situation and deduce, "This is safe," "This is dangerous," "This is risky," "This is good," or "This is bad."

It will then send a message directly to your hypothalamus, which will consequently begin flooding your body with billions of neural peptides. (These little chemicals are hormones that link up with every cell in your body, and they trigger deep feelings at every level—psychologically, emotionally, and physiologically.)

So, with all of his neurons, emotions, and hormones flaring, how do you think little Billy now feels about not spilling milk? He feels anxiety, fear, and stress. Plus, since his brain doesn't link emotion to the word "don't," all it really hears and translates physiologically is "spill the milk."

Plus, this metaphor gets even worse if little Billy is an overachiever. As an overachiever, Billy won't just think of 50 ways to spill milk and avoid them, he will think of 200 ways to not spill the milk. As Billy walks over to the counter to get the milk, he'll look skyward and think, "A meteor could come through the ceiling and rip the pitcher out of my hands. Oh my gosh, now I need to worry about meteors!"

If you're like a lot of my clients, there is a lot of transformation awaiting you with this new realization because of all this will play out down the road.

What does this type of mindset mean to Billy as an adult? Here's what happens—when little Billy grows up, instead of "don't spill the milk," Billy translates the word "success" into "don't screw up," "don't lose this business," or "don't get this person mad."

And unfortunately, by projecting those thoughts, Billy will draw those unintended results towards him.

What if Billy's parents had instead told him, "Billy, pour the milk *carefully*"?

Instead of thinking about ways to spill it, Billy's brain would have started coming up with 50 ways to be careful. Maybe he would have thought, "I'll use two hands," "I'll pour slowly," or "I'll use a big glass." Then, instead of feeling nervous, stressed, and anxious, Billy would have felt successful after pouring a spotless glass of milk!

And, what will happen when *this* version of Billy grows up? He won't be trained to sabotage himself, he will be well practiced in giving himself positive commands, and he'll tell himself things like, "I am going to prepare so I succeed on this sales call," and "I am going to plan a special evening so I can create a magical moment with my wife."

This is the science behind New Age manifestation and neural linguistics. Focus on what you want, and you will create it at a higher level; focus on what you *don't* want, and you will make it a reality.

The good news is that regardless of your current thinking, you have the power to change it.

Which leads me to...

Myth 7: Is the glass half empty or half full?

Finally, the last myth. I mentioned this concept briefly in the last chapter, however, I want to go a little bit deeper. As I explained before, the glass is *neither* half full nor half empty—it is always both in every person. But, there is actually a quantum aspect to this question that even furthers this point.

As Einstein proved, light can be both a wave and a particle because it has both properties. Thus, energy itself is multi-dimensional. However, when you test energy as a particle, it has properties of a particle, whereas if you test it as a wave, it has completely different properties. The components inside energy can simultaneously be different and the same. Although this concept contradicts linear physical science as we know it, it is proven reality.

With this quantum revelation in mind, if I were to give you a glass filled up exactly to the halfway point and ask you, "Is that glass half full? Or is it half empty?" Everybody would know what the answer *should be*, however, you might still insist, "It's half full." Or, as research indicates, most of you would say, "It's half empty."

But, the truth is, it is always, always *both* simultaneously.

The real question is, "Are *you* half full or half empty?" If you observe your life as half full, you'll experience it as half full; if you observe life as half empty, you'll experience it as half empty. We all bounce back and forth between these two spectrums because life is always half full when you feel successful and when everything is going as planned. However, the key to experiencing true fulfillment is to see that life is also full when the chips are down. It's the intense and critical times in your life that provide profound opportunities. I know this is another counterintuitive shift, but if you want to bring the "old you" to another level, the time for the "new you" to show up is when it's hardest to appear.

Don't just try harder. Commit to making a deeper shift.

Throughout this book, you're going to learn to live in an extremely deep place where you'll welcome crisis as the moment when your greatest growth can occur. Letting go of each of these seven myths is the first step.

So, the new question is...

- Who is the "old you"?

- Why?

- How are you going to be different?

- If you answer that question truthfully, do you like the answer?

CHAPTER THREE:
The Delusions

Stop labeling yourself based on past actions.
Either change your actions or change the psychology
that creates your actions. Who you are is up to you.

In order for you to be wildly successful, you need to root out every lie and every disguised bad character trait pretending to love and help you. You need to shine a light on the illusions that are blocking you so they scurry away like the cockroaches they are.

This chapter is about revealing your deepest delusions. These are clever and intricately camouflaged poisons that challenge the way you think about your successes and your failures. These paradigms work very, very hard to look and act like your friend. They are subtle and powerful as they whisper disparaging comments to you. Sometimes they even yell to get your attention. And, if that doesn't work, they're not above using blackmail to control you. Trust me, these illusions are *not* your friends— they are _de_lusions. Here are six to look out for.

Delusion #1: Failure with Honor

Have you ever heard the phrase "failing with honor"? When you fail with honor, it means "Well I didn't succeed, but I still feel pretty good about it."

This *sounds* like a noble ideal. There is definitely honor in accepting failure and learning from it. However, the concept of "failure with honor" has some hidden meanings. Let me explain.

Do you remember the famous scene in "Star Wars" when Yoda says, "Do or do not—there is no try"?

What was Yoda really saying? What does it mean to not try, but to *do*?

During my coaching sessions, I hear the word "try" a lot. Clients will often say to me, "Oh, Bill I am trying *so hard* to change. I really am *trying*."

Take a moment and try this exercise—put a pen on ground and then *try* to pick it up. Go ahead, set the book aside and try it.

If you still have your pen in your hand, you haven't followed the instructions. I don't want you to *actually* pick it up—I just want you to *try*.

Does this make sense? *Trying* is code for *not doing*. It's an excuse, an illusion, and a mental block that stymies progress. If you are someone who "tries" to do something, you likely also say things like, "Probably I'll get it," "Maybe I'll get it," or "Well, sometimes I can get it and other times I can't."

All of these comments are really saying, "Half of me is moving forward; half of me isn't. Part of me is doing, part of me isn't. I'm *trying*."

This is what it means to "fail with honor," and the only way you can move forward is to reverse this pattern. I want you to be able to wake up tomorrow and take off like a rocket ship, but first you need to eliminate this psychology from your databank forever.

Next…

Delusion #2: How vs. Why

I hear this comment from my clients, as well, "I really like you, Bill. I get it, but you know, I don't see *how* this is going to work for me," (strong emphasis on the how). "In order for me to feel good, safe, and certain in this process, I have to understand *how* it's all going to work."

So many people struggle with this mindset. "How do I change?" and "*How* do I get that outcome?"

Even though you know changing will help your present circumstances, you feel more certain about your "old you" patterns and hang-ups. Even if the "old you" is not perfect or even okay, at least you know what to do, *how* it feels, and what to expect.

Well, here's what you need to know. Successful people aren't wired this way. They never care about the *how* first. Instead, they focus solely on the *why*. They know if they really want and have a compelling enough reason to get their outcome, *it will happen*. End of story. When you know the why and the why is big enough, your mind will create, find, associate, discover, and construct your desired result.

Some of us can only relate to this driven, focused mindset in dire circumstances. For example, suppose you have unsuccessfully been "trying" to stop smoking for years when something suddenly made it absolutely mandatory—you got pregnant. All of a sudden, you then had a very big *why*, and the *how* became irrelevant. You simply threw your cigarettes away and stopped.

Other life changes can be just as simple and straight-forward. In fact, you can do *anything* in a single instant as long as you have a big enough *why*. What have you been "trying" to do? Make more money? Get a better job? Find your soul mate?

Why?

Make a list and dig really deep on this. WHY? What will it mean to you? How will it feel? What will your life look like afterwards?

The why is all that really matters. The how always will fall into place. And, the more intense the why, the easier the how will become.

This is especially important to remember during hard times in your life. During those tough storms, most people falter. They give up. They believe they're on the right track when it feels easy, but they lose sight of their vision and disassociate from the deep meaning behind their desires once it's tough. No matter what comes your way, just remember to focus on the *why* first, and... everything else will come!

Start playing a movie script in your mind. Start seeing yourself starring in the life you desire and really *feel* the experience. In order to see results, you must fully associate to something that deeply excites you. Superficial goals won't work. If you say to yourself, "Well, I really should be more successful because um, well, I really would like to upgrade my house, I love my spouse, and I kind of want more for my kids," you won't get very far. It isn't enough. You're going to have to dig deeper and know what you *really* want to move forward.

You also will need to keep track of what are you doing in the "now" in order to get there.

Delusion #3: Now vs. Not Now

It's nice to have a vision, but you need to focus on what you can do today in the "now" because your daily actions are what will ultimately drive your future. Let me explain. If you are like most people, you see the world in three frames—the past, the present, and the future. You have a past, you remember it, and it is real to you. You live in the present, it's certainly real, and you do the best you can. And, you have a future—you have a dream, a vision, and goals. This seems pretty logical and straight-forward, right? Well, it's not. There's more, and I am going to challenge you to think beyond this three-dimensional world because your reality actually *only* exists in two frames.

This is how it works. Psychologically, you can think, remember, feel, and focus on three dimensions. You may use verbs to describe what happens in all three timeframes. However, in terms of what you create and do in life, there is only "now" and "not now."

Think about it. What happened in the past is nothing more than a quantum blip. The past exists only in little packets of electricity that run around in a neural net within your brain. But, it's no longer real. Now, the *meaning* you created about past events is important, but only because it affects the way you handle the present.

I like to tell a joke about an American who goes down to Mexico for a work project. However, in order to fulfill his business obligation, he has to get a required permit. So, each day, he goes into the local government office and asks to get his paperwork processed, and every day the bureaucrat behind the desk tells him, "Oh, I'm sorry—mañana."

After repeating this exact process for five days straight, the man finally gets frustrated and asks the agent why he keeps telling him to come back "tomorrow" if the papers *still* won't be ready, and the agent replies, "Oh, that's your mistake, my friend. Mañana doesn't really mean 'tomorrow'; it means *'not today.'*"

Take a moment and really think about this. When you are busy creating a future and thinking about how much you *would like to* change, are you really making any progress? Or, are you more like the frustrating agent in the story above, continually telling yourself "mañana" (not today) as your life passes you by?

In order for you to really change your future, you *must* do the opposite. You must go to the *'now'* matrix. Sometime during your day today, try this—during a conversation with a co-worker, friend, or loved one, try adding the word "now" and "not now" after a statement. For example, you might say, "I'm going to wash the car now," and then later, you might say to your boss, "I'm going to get that report to you, but not now."

Can you feel the difference in these two statements? One triggers a sense of ownership and presence; the other may or may not *ever* happen.

This is your reality. What you do in the "now" is what creates who you are. What you do in the "not now" is what you desire, but don't actualize. We comfort ourselves by saying, "Well, in the future, I'll do 'x' or 'y'," "In the future, I'll lose weight," "In the future, I'll stop smoking," "In the future, I'll have this incredible relationship."

But, in order to make your future vision real, at some point you have to ask yourself, "Am I going to do my future *now*?"

Think about this for a moment. What if, as you smoked a cigarette, you could literally see a tumor growing on your chest? Then, as soon as you stopped, you could see the tumor start disappearing? If this were reality, *no one* would smoke. The consequences would be in the "now" timeframe, and you would receive instant gratification for stopping.

Unfortunately, that's not how it works. Every action we take still has an impact—we just cannot physically see it until some time down the road, and as a result, we procrastinate. We think to ourselves, "In the future,

I'll solve this problem," "Tomorrow, I'll be better," "Maybe next week, I'll start working out."

What happens to the New Year's resolutions you make every January? If you are like most people, you go year after year and continue to make the same annual resolution again and again.

I have something important to tell you—making plans to do something even a short time into the future is a delusion. YOUR "IMAGINARY" FUTURE WILL NEVER COME!

You must start living and creating in the "now."

You must also break old patterns that keep you in the past.

Delusion #4: Conscious Consciousness

Have you ever heard of "Johari's Window?"

This is a common psychiatric tool created by Joseph Luft and Harry Ingham. It was designed to help people understand how they relate to the world around them. However, the concept can also be applied to how we learn and process skills and information.

Basically, there are two crucial axes to learning—conscious versus unconscious and competence versus incompetence. Here's how it works. When you learn a complex task, you work very hard to learn the steps. You practice each component deliberately until you perfect it, and at that point, you've "learned" it.

For example, if you were a piano teacher or golf coach, you might allocate months or even years to learn and master certain skills. Perhaps you would even get so good you could perform your expertise in your sleep. This would make you "unconsciously competent."

Similarly, the "old you" is "unconsciously competent" in how you handle life. The "old you" has patterns, excuses, stories, modalities, and fall-backs that occur naturally, without thinking. In fact, this part of you is *so* well-practiced in its routines you don't even realize the actions you take aren't actually yours.

As a result, anytime you try to change or start to improve, it feels a bit awkward. Discovering a new way to interact with life is just like learning to play the piano or honing your golf swing—the subtle nuances feel strange and clumsy at first. However, you can't give up just because it's new. You have to work at it until you have it down. This is the only way to master *any* skill, including discovering *The Inevitable You*®.

You can expect additional discomfort down the road, as well. Even if you are a well-practiced professional, something you can usually do with ease can become challenging under the right conditions. Should you increase the stakes, you may have to stretch all over again—regardless of how good you are. You could be a completely competent singer and still be anxious when performing at Carnegie Hall.

Whatever your scenario, I can guarantee whatever you dislike about yourself, you've practiced it a million times. Consequently, you are now so good at it, you can do it seamlessly and with little thought. In fact, even when you try to improve, as soon as you get uncomfortable, have a bad day, get into an argument, or disappoint your boss, you probably fall back to what you're used to. It's not that you enjoy feeling miserable, that's just where your experience lies. But unfortunately, the moment you fall back is the point where you give up on yourself and consequently remain stuck. You think, "Oh, I can't do this. It doesn't work. I'll never be able to do *this.*"

Today you can change that. Realize the changes and growth you desire are not a rocket scientist's tasks. However, also know that it does take some time to weave new behavior into your life's tapestry. Plus, if you are just now beginning to grasp this concept, your change will be proportionally incremental and progressive. It won't happen right away, and you will not be able to relish in instant gratification. To expect otherwise is to set yourself up for failure.

The application of this concept is so broad and multi-faceted that I am going to touch more on it later. For now, just know that your problem is likely embedded into your psyche in both conscious and unconscious ways.

Moving on... This next delusion is perhaps the most damaging...

Delusion #5: Sabotage

Sabotage is a virtual lockbox. It can keep you paralyzed, insecure, and miserable—it's disturbingly invasive.

Like a governor on an engine, sabotage limits the speed of your motivation and serves as a thermostat of sorts. As soon as your car (or self growth) gets too hot, it shuts off.

That said—sabotage is not your enemy. It actually has altruistic intentions meant to protect you. It feeds on your safety and security and would sacrifice *everything* in order to maintain that ideal. But, it's protecting a primitive version of you that's driven by your ego. When a storm rolls into your life, sabotage is the *how* and the *why* you'll take the sails down, quit the race, and head back into the harbor.

It's not that you're broken or stupid. We all fall back sometimes. Sabotage simply stems from a delusion that you need to protect yourself from failure. However, here's what sabotage doesn't realize—failure is laden with inherent benefits. While sabotage moves towards limitation, failure moves towards success.

Sabotage deludes you into thinking you can't do something. It slows down your speed when you think life is too risky. It feels like a safety net, but it's really holding you back. It's the "half-empty" (and equally destructive) side to "failing with honor."

Are you with me?

Similarly, the next delusion also holds you back, but in an even more subtle way.

Delusion #6: That Old Song on the Radio

This one works as a sort of mental loop, and it can trip you up regardless of your present success and capability—for no apparent reason at all. Scientists call this phenomenon a "neural trap."

Here's how it works. Because your brain is so smart, it can process familiar "notes" to a "song" or life experience in less than three nanoseconds, and the more you do something, the faster it recognizes patterns from the past. In fact, your brain will actually hardwire experiences in your brain and link them to emotional conclusions.

But, here's where it gets tricky—those conclusions may not always relate to your present situation. Your brain will trigger a response so quickly you probably will not even realize what happened. All of sudden, you'll feel bad for no apparent reason and not know what to make of it.

It's just like the emotions triggered by an old song on the radio.

Have you ever been driving down the road thinking about your day when an old break-up song from your teens starts playing? Suddenly, you're back on a beach, feeling an intense broken heart, smelling the salt in the air, and feeling just as bad as you did the day of an old summer romance break-up. Then, for no good reason, all of sudden, you are consequently sad, depressed, and lonely.

But, you're not really upset. Nothing has actually happened... it's *just* an old song on the radio.

While running this pattern, most people don't even know why they're upset. They probably don't even make the connection between the trigger and the past experience. So, they ask themselves, "Why don't I feel good right now?"

And, since they asked, their brains will work to give them an answer. "Well, you don't feel good because of your health, because of your boring job, because..., because..., because..."

Your brain will work hard to give you numerous plausible answers to any question you ask, and it will start stacking the conclusions until you can justify your feelings. Yet, the answers will likely have absolutely *nothing* to do with your present condition.

By the end of this book, y*ou're going to put a new song in your mind*. You're going to shift your old patterns and step back into control.

Life is not in control of you.

So, now that you have a grasp of the invasive delusions that can hold you back, take some time to associate to a powerful vision that can help you overcome these obstacles.

Remember, if your "why" is big enough, you will figure out the "how" no matter what.

- What is your <u>why</u>?

- Why do you <u>really</u> want to be successful?

- Why do you want to be the extraordinary, magical, *Inevitable You*®?

CHAPTER FOUR:
Fear, Failure & Inescapable Conclusions

You are not perfect yet at being "not perfect."

Are you noticing that many of the things that seem to "help you" are actually holding you back?

Besides delusions and myths, there are just a few more roadblocks keeping the "old you" stuck, and I've saved some of the best for last. This chapter is about the most common and pervasive hurdles we face and what you can do to combat them.

First...

Change the Way You Think of Fear

I'd like to give you a new perspective on fear. What is it exactly? Does it hold you back? Does it energize you? Is it half empty or half full? At its core, *what is fear?*

The answer? It's all of the above and even more. It can energize you, protect you, give you perspective, control you, and hold you back. Like so many other things in life, it is *both* half empty and half full.

Have you ever heard this expression that defines fear as this acronym— False Evidence Appearing Real? Take a moment and really ponder this phrase for a moment. *False Evidence Appearing Real*. When people say "I'm not succeeding," "I'm not successful," "I can't," or "I don't," they are actually telling you about their fears.

If you ask them, "*Why* are you not successful," or "*Why* don't you give it a shot," they will tell you, "Well, I'm afraid of failing," "I'm afraid of success," and "I'm afraid of rejection."

But, 99 percent of the time, those reasons are not the real source of their inner conflict. There's always something else lurking deep behind those superficial fears.

Here's what is really going on.

People create these explanations because they are even more afraid they will not be able to solve their *real* conflict. Their deeper fears are, "Will I be able to have control over my life," "Will the people I love still care about and respect me if I fail," and "Will I be enough?"

I'm going to ask you to look at your fears through a new lens. I want you take them on as *The Inevitable You®* so you can be strong enough to see what's really happening. There is a reason why you are still holding onto them, and here's a clue—how do your fears *benefit* you?

Many successful clients will show up for a session and tell me, "Bill, I'm afraid of failure." To which I respond, "What have you ever failed at?" And they say, "Well, um, well... I've never failed at anything."

I then ask, "Are you *really* afraid of failure, or do you use fear of failure as a form of motivational energy that drives you?"

This will usually create a look of confusion followed by one of understanding on their faces.

Because here's the truth—fear *always* serves a purpose. There is always a benefit. Otherwise, you wouldn't invite it into your life. In fact, the *real* fear is using the gift of your imagination to create things you don't want.

You don't actually fear *failure*; you fear your creative vision of what failure *could bring*, but in doing so, you are forgetting that in order to be great, *you have to fail*. With great success comes great failure.

I will also admit—*sometimes* fear can be smart and righteous. Sometimes it is completely appropriate. When gold-medal skier Picabo Street gets on top of an icy triple black-diamond Olympic run with four years of training on the line—it's completely appropriate for her to feel fear. When Picabo stares down at that snowy, stark incline, of *course* she is afraid. However, instead of cowering to the fear, she actually *uses* it in that moment to her advantage. That's what makes her different. That's what champions do. They look at fear as an opportunity to mark the edge. They turn the "empty" side of fear into "full" by accessing the power it provides. In that defining moment of release, fear becomes a co-creator in life. It declares, "Oh, you better be afraid; you'd better be firing all cylinders right now; you'd better be 100 percent alive."

In this sense, fear is actually the adrenaline of life, the fuel of courage, and the nectar of greatness. But, in order to get there, you can't fall back. The precise moment when you feel fear is exactly when you need to gather the best of *everything you've got* to charge forward.

Martial artists understand this principle. When faced with an opponent rushing towards him, a skilled martial artist will not shield himself, scream, or push back. Instead, he will artfully embrace his opponent. He will understand and abide by this universal law—what you push in life, pushes back. The more you resist that which you don't want, the more it persists.

By embracing an opponent, a martial artist can deflect his energy and send it in a more advantageous direction. He will actually embrace his opponents, align with them, bring them closer, deflect them, and then send them in the opposite direction.

Maybe you already know this.

But, even if you already "get" this concept and have great intentions about embracing your fears, when you are tested in a new way that personally challenges *you*, it's really hard to find your greatness. You will have to focus on putting it into practice when it *really* matters. And, that will be *exactly* the moment when you have the opportunity to do something remarkable. *That is your moment to seize and conquer what's standing in your way.*

The key is to embrace your challenges and to see the opportunity behind them. If you resist, push away, or fight them, you'll only give your fear more power. Instead, be grateful for how fear serves you. See it as a signal to step up, a call to action, and an invitation to fully experience life.

Fear is such a phenomenal place from which to grow, but in order to use your fear to your advantage, you need to learn how to redirect it.

Put Fear to Work for You

You're going to have to figure out the strategy or recipe you use to create fear so that you can then tweak the pattern in a more empowering way.

Let me explain.

I often do a "stop-smoking" session where I can take absolutely any client who signs up and get him to stop smoking in one to two hours. Sounds bold, right? Trust me—it is. I definitely face many challenges in the process. People paying to quit will often give me the many reasons why they will be the one "exception" to my process.

But, here's how it usually works. First, I start by asking my clients to list the benefits smoking gives them. Some will say, "Well, there are no benefits. I just can't quit. It's ruining my life. I have cancer, I can't smell anymore, I can't taste my food... blah, blah, blah."

So, to that, I ask, "What *could be good* about being a smoker?"

And, this is when the conversation gets more interesting.

"Well, let's see. You get to leave your cubicle, leave your office, go outside, and socialize with other smokers regularly throughout the day. There is also the manual dexterity satisfaction that comes with fondling your cigarette—not to mention the oral gratification that goes with it."

Eventually, once we get going, my patient and I will usually come up with at least 12 to 15 smoking benefits. And, once a patient has owned the fact that he is getting something out of smoking, *that's* when I know I will be able to figure out a way to get him to stop.

It's not our *conscious* brain that makes change difficult, it's the *unconscious* subsidiary benefits that mess us up. As a result, the *best* way to stop smoking is to define the benefits that a bad habit gives you and then to figure out how to fulfill those needs in a healthier way.

Make sense?

Good—because similarly, the secret to conquering your fears is to get to the true core of how they serve you (which requires an intense amount of honesty on your part), and to learn how to meet those needs in a more empowering way. You need to create a new strategy that matches or exceeds the benefits the fear brings you.

And, once you know how to appreciate and dance with your fears, you'll also need to...

Appreciate Your Failures

Most people avoid failure *at all costs*. There is so much negative meaning and attachment to the notion of failing that most people will say anything, do anything, and create anything (even if it makes no sense), in order to avoid feeling like a failure. They will deny, blame, create accusations, denounce uncontrollable, outside forces, and become defensive in order to deflect failure. They may also claim disinterest, pretend they don't really care, and become dismissive.

But, worst of all, in the dark soul of the night, a person hiding from failure secretly hates or loathes himself. He beats himself up and says things like, "I have no will power," "I have no discipline," "I'm doomed to be this person," and "I've given up."

We also have societal language patterns that try to hide failure. We'll say things like, "I've made a mistake," "I've made an error," "Oops, that's a blooper!", "I *miscalculated*," "That was a faux pas, a misstep, a blunder, an oversight...."

From now on, as soon as you hear yourself saying any of these phrases, notice how they contribute to your "failure with honor programming." Using these phrases enables us to keep a distinct balance between what we have, what we want, and what we're most afraid of, but it also holds us back from diving in, taking risks, experiencing failure, and *using* those lessons to succeed wildly.

I'm not saying it will be easy. Society often goes against you on this one. For instance, most large companies will *say* that they *encourage* mistakes because it leads to innovation. However, unfortunately, most don't really follow through on this commitment. When was the last time your boss praised your mistakes and deemed them as "innovative"?

It's a huge mixed message and challenge we face as a society.

But, that's an entirely different book, and another conversation.

Here's onto another big hurdle. In order to step into the "new you," you must also be able to...

Diffuse Inescapable Conclusions

Your brain is not only a powerful databank and processor; it is also a remarkably creative storyteller. In fact, in order to understand and relate to the world around us, we constantly create labels to categorize people, places, and ideas. We develop stories to relay our experiences, and replay vivid movies in our minds to reinforce our identity.

This is something that *all humans* do. It's our nature, and it's part of what has made us the adaptable and progressive creators we are.

However, most people write their personal screenplay, cast their characters, and even create their final movie *unknowingly*. Their story is based on their past, they allow other people to cast the show *for them*, and they continually play *and replay* a disempowering movie in their minds.

How unfortunate is that?

You must take in this statement (and really feel it in your heart)—*you and only you* have the ability to create your own story, to become the leading hero, and to stand at the gateway of your mind so as to only welcome those thoughts, ideas, and movies that will serve you and your dreams.

In fact, this is how you are truly *meant* to live. Your brain is not equipped with multitudes of creativity so that you can beat yourself up, shoot down your dreams, and record failures; it's designed to create a vision so powerful that you can literally see *through* any obstacles placed in your path.

It's just that the "old you" never learned how to use this power. The "old you" allowed your ego and fears to take control... and you probably don't even realize it.

For example, think about a child who grew up poor and hating life. He probably told himself over and over again as he became an adult, "I'll never be poor," "I'll never be poor," "I'll *never* be poor!"

So then, he grew up and started to work— guess what? He's *not* poor. In fact, he's so afraid of being poor that he has amassed an extremely large amount of wealth. *But, it's still not enough.* There is probably not any *sum* of money that can stop his hunger for more. So, when will he finally be happy and fulfilled? He won't! Not until he figures out the deeper labels, stories, and movies behind his real desires. This is the <u>only</u> way he will be able to understand his motives and gain control of the script.

To help make this all more relatable, let's go into each of the elements a little deeper.

Labels

Are you a victim, a survivor, or a champion?

If your story includes elements of trauma or you've been criminalized in your past, you probably have defined yourself as a victim. If this is the case, you've probably never had what you want and always suffered.

But, here's an interesting thing—some people who experience horrific acts of violence or injury don't associate to being a victim at all. They call themselves a *survivor*. They say, "I survived that. I got stronger. I got better. I may not be perfect or have all the things that I want. I may not have the same capabilities I did before the trauma, *but I survived it.*" That's their focus, story, and belief.

There's also an even smaller percentage of people at the upper end of the bell curve who actually take their horrible experience and define themselves as a *champion* for having overcome it. For example, someone who was molested as a child might go on to create a huge program to protect other children from abuse. Or, someone diagnosed with testicular cancer might use that information to fuel a passion for cycling and become a seven-time Tour de France champion. Champions are people who take their deepest challenge and connect it to their deepest greatness.

Here's the bottom line—trauma does not create victims, survivors, or champions. *You do.* This is the power of your mind. This is how powerful the labels you create become. How you define and choose to remember any life experience is completely up to you.

Stories

It doesn't stop there. Do you have a story about who you are, how you got there, and what life means?

And, by the way, if you're suffering right now, you need to know that I don't want you to think I am diminishing or dismissing your pain, but *this* *is your opportunity to escape the bondage created from that trauma and to release it <u>forever</u>.*

The stories you tell yourself and others about who you are, why you are, and why you don't have what you want are the reality you live every day. This is what makes a story an "inescapable conclusion." When you live a story, talk about it, and breathe it, you and the story become one.

Here are some examples, "Ever since I lost my job, I haven't had a good night of sleep," "I can't work because I am tired all the time," or "My heart is so broken, I can't focus on anything else."

Your "story" is something you constantly share with friends (or even strangers), and you probably have multiple versions of it. When life gets intense and hard, your story is right by your side to rationalize all of the unfortunate difficulties in your life.

But, as you let go of the "old you" and get closer to understanding the "new you," I'd like to ask you—are those stories really true? Are they really who you are? Do you believe that you can change them?

You can.

Here's how it works.

All stories start with a hero who has a noble desire. That hero faces certain challenges in order to reach his goal. He must face an opponent of some sort who makes his task seem insurmountable (the bigger the opponent, the greater the hero, by the way.) He comes up with a plan to conquer his opponent, goes to battle, and through the process realizes his deeper needs which creates equilibrium in his life.

All stories have this formula. It's classic Literature 101. Seeing a hero overcome a challenge and step into his true identity is something we all crave and love. It's why we spend 10 dollars to go to the movies on a regular basis, why we love novels, and why we watch "reality" TV. You just have to connect the dots—*you* are the hero of your own movie and *you* have the power to overcome your own opponents—internally, externally, and intimately.

Now, for some clients this explanation isn't enough. They like to give me a variety of reasons why their "story" is different. "I have clinical depression," "I am in a wheelchair," "I have dyslexia," or "I don't have any money," are some of the excuses I get.

I really do want to empathize with all these challenges. I'm not diminishing the unique and personal hurdles you may face in any way, but that challenge is not why you are who you are.

Does this make sense?

Remember—the bigger the challenge, the bigger the hero. The difficulties in your life only give you an even greater chance to make a bigger difference in this world.

Don't you think it's time to rewrite *your* story?

Mental Movies

So, now that you know how your "stories" affect you, you're also going to want to film a few new movies. Think about it—do you ever *not* have a movie playing in your mind? While driving to work, what are you picturing? While worrying about an appointment, what movie is playing in your head? While thinking about your kids, what do you envision?

On the other hand, while thinking about an upcoming date, what do you see? When you're looking forward to an easy Friday in the office, what do you visualize?

Notice how the movie shifts. Unfortunately, most of your movies are probably about fear, uncertainty, and doubt. You play these movies often, and they are much more animated than your empowering selections. This is unfortunate. The more you focus on the negative aspects of your challenge, the louder and more illuminated they become. In fact, doing so will make the villain seem *huge* and the challenges much larger than they actually are. Everything will start to seem insurmountable and impossible to overcome. As you continue to visualize this reoccurring horror film in your mind, the volume will get even louder, the scenes will get even bigger and brighter, and you will begin to embody the movie to the point of genuine physical pain.

Meanwhile, your empowering movie will linger somewhere in the background of your mind—muted, distant, and faded.

Why are you making yourself suffer? I mean, how many times do you go back and re-watch a bad movie? More than once? More than 10,000 times? More than a million times? Would you even stay to the end of a bad movie? Would you like to *change* the bad ending if you could?

It's time to wake up and rewrite the movie of your life. And, when the old, bad movie comes on again... *eject it!* Mute the sound, move it far into the distance where you can hardly see it and all the characters, especially the bad guys, sound like a bunch of Disney characters.

Then, when the good movie plays, watch it in Technicolor, turn up the volume, and play it over and over again. See the happy, perfect ending and let that feeling resonate through your entire body.

Remember, *you* get to write the screenplay, *you're* the director, and *you* add the special effects.

What do you want your world to be like?

Wired to Win!

This chapter marks the END of the "old you."

You are no longer wired for failure. You life is no longer about avoiding mistakes and challenges.

If you apply all the concepts we've discussed so far into your day-to-day life, you are wired to SUCCEED.

But, if you are still not convinced, if you are still looking for ways to *avoid failure*, I have to tell you this mindset will only serve to minimize potential pain. It won't move you forward.

I recently had a client really argue this point with me. "But Bill," he said, "If I figure out every contingency, analyze everything that can go wrong, and put a solution in place, isn't that guaranteeing me success?"

It was painful for me to even hear him say this! Can you imagine how painful his life is? Oh, he has some "success," and if you could see me now, I just gave it the two finger air quotes around the word "success." Even retelling his "story" exhausts me!

If you have any thoughts of this nature still lingering—TRUST ME, it's time to let them go. "The old you" is a primitive form of unconscious programming. It is *not you.*

Let's move forward.

You are now programmed for greatness, and any step backwards is by choice.

- So, what has been your story?

- What was your fear?

- What was the benefit of this fear?

- Why must you change NOW?

- What would it feel like for you to believe that failure is <u>required</u> to succeed?

- How are you wired to win?

PART 2:

The "New You"

WILLIAM SUMNER

CHAPTER FIVE:
Transitional Thinking

Turn the light on.

Congratulations. You've opened the door to an *entirely new world*.

If you are like most people, you're probably feeling at least somewhat overwhelmed.

However great it feels to know that you're heading in the right direction, it is also likely more than a little intimidating and scary.

You can see that there is a vast new landscape in front of you, but the road ahead may appear dark and uncertain. You don't know what to expect. *This is normal.* You are now venturing into the unknown, and you are shifting the path of your current trajectory. You are probably asking yourself, "Where am I going, and more importantly, *where will I end up*?"

No matter how uncertain you feel, just know that you don't have to make this harder than it is. Sometimes all you have to do in order to make a shift is *turn the bus around*. Sometimes simply turning around and shifting your perspective is *all it takes* to see a new horizon and to approach your challenges from a more powerful position. Changing your vantage point can give you the ability to see solutions that didn't seem to exist before.

And, even if you don't move very far at first, you're still making progress. *Every* single day that you take even one small step in a new direction creates momentum that can boost your confidence. Sometimes it may *feel* like no progress at all, and sometimes it may even feel like two steps backwards. Regardless, just know that none of that matters when you have a positive focal point.

Knowing all that you now do about the "old you," all it takes is one small shift to embark on a new way of being. Simply *turn your bus around*, and everything will begin to change. You do not need to have all the answers at this stage; you do *not* even need to have a solid plan in place. You are not seeking perfection right now; you are simply seeking momentum and change.

Take control of the wheel, know that you can *choose* the direction, and then *take one step forward*. The path to get from where you are to *there* may be daunting, and that's okay. Don't let the uncertainty stymie your progress. Don't get stuck here and revert back to your comfort zone. Simply expect some temporary unease as you feel the transition, and give yourself permission to live without the expectation of knowing. Keep your head down and keep driving.

Here's what will happen.

Your movement will create momentum. Even if you have to push forward a few times to get there, you'll feel yourself finally start to break free of your old ruts. You'll begin to embody new thought patterns, you'll start to employ new tools, and you'll start to feel a calming new sense of hope in life…

So, let's do it.

At this point, take in this sentence again—*ALL results begin with a thought.*

I know I asked you this before, but only the "old you" was previously listening. On a scale of 1 to 10, 10 being "rock solid," how much do you *really* believe this statement? Before you move on, this statement *must* be a 10. Stop here and ponder this idea as long as you need to until you can accept its truth.

You control reality.

Your trajectory is now pointing towards a magnificent future that you may have given up on—until now.

The Act After the Act

Clients often challenge me on the notion that all results begin with a thought. People will say to me, "Bill, I didn't get into that car wreck because I *thought* about it beforehand," or "I didn't lose my home and my family to a tsunami because of my *mindset.*"

Well, I'm not talking about the *events* you experience in life. I'm talking about *how you handle them* and *what you make of their meaning.* Your reality is not based on the *event* itself, "good" or "bad"—it's what you do *afterwards* that matters. This is where you choose either pain or progress.

I call this the "act after the act." Most people believe that certain activities in life either give them pain or pleasure. When the act is good, life is good. When the act is bad, life is bad. Seems plain and simple, right? Well, it doesn't work that way.

Here's what really happens. During the "act after the act," you get to *choose* your response. After a car wreck, after you lose your job, or after you buy a winning lottery ticket, <u>you</u> get to *pick* the next act. *You* get to choose. You can set yourself up to win by letting the most powerful possible version of you do the honors. Or, you can fall back into old patterns and let the unevolved part of yourself make decisions. It's up to you. Whatever you decide, I can tell you one thing—as you begin to change your thinking and make new choices, you will start to notice *new results.* If you so choose, you have the ultimate power to step into the greatest possible version of you.

Remember: You Are Inevitable

Remember when I told you that you have *unlimited potential?* Do you also remember having a hard time accepting this about yourself? That was the "old you." The "new you" is not limited in this way. The "new you" understands whole-heartedly that life is by your design. The "new you" knows your greatest opportunities are disguised as challenges. The "new you" finds strength in pain and relishes in your future vision. The "new you" sees what's possible, not what's already happened.

It's time to get excited!

You are about to reclaim the unlimited being that you have always been and are designed to be. This is who your four-year-old self knew and understood you to be. All four-year-old children are at the pinnacle of their power. They believe in themselves, they believe in their ability to live life at a ten, and they spend time thinking about success, not failure.

But, getting back to this ideal requires emotional mastery. Can you trigger positive emotions on command? Can you shift a bad attitude into an aura of gratitude in a single instant?

Fulfillment requires discipline; failure does not. If you want to be miserable, misery would love to have your company. There are plenty of people who will help you wallow in your pain.

You'll have all the friends you want when you're sad, depressed, and miserable. It's curious how choosing greatness will likely challenge many of those around you. Once you start to select optimism in spite of obstacles, once you start to embody powerful, positive emotions, and once you start to get excited about *everything* that life presents, people around you may start to question you. "Oh, Mr. Happy, what are you so happy about? What do you have to be happy about?" they'll say.

Your friends may even pick on you, challenge you, and push against you. It's not because you're wrong, it's not because they're bad people, and it's not because they don't think you will succeed—it's because watching you be happy in the face of a challenge or a problem forces them to reevaluate what makes *them* comfortable in their own life. It forces them to look at their own inadequacies, and so it's easier for them if you are just as miserable as they are.

But, you can't let others hold you back. Being miserable will only bring you (and them) more misery. And, the more you focus on negative thoughts and misery, the more emotions you'll feel around the experience, which will only intensify your challenges exponentially. (Remember—emotions catalyze the power of the thought. They are the lighter fluid that ignites the entire process.)

Now that you understand this, I want you to do two things *right now*. First, resolve to *stop* asking yourself miserable questions. Stop asking, "Why don't I have...?" and "Why can't I...?" questions. When you ask these ridiculously bad, poor, tough, mean-spirited questions, your brain will work to find you an answer, and it will not be uplifting.

Second, I want you to *start* asking yourself better questions like, "What's right with me?' or "How can I solve this problem?"

No matter how bad your life (or any part of it) may seem, there is always a silver lining. There is always something positive with which to work, but you'll only be able to see it if you ask yourself better questions.

Remember... *you are inevitable.* Remember your power. Remember your potential. This is a truth you recognize deep within.

Your Unconscious Knows

I don't care what silo of thinking, school of thought, or philosophy you come from, when it comes to this world of potential, all roads lead to the same place. Whether you follow Dale Carnegie or Zig Ziglar, whether you believe in quantum physics or religious studies, and whether you are new age or old world, it all relies on the same core principles—your faith and focus. Although your conscious mind controls and comprehends your day-to-day actions, it's your unconscious mind that really drives the show. There are deeper parts of you that your conscious brain doesn't understand. There are parts of yourself that your brain does not see and hear, yet your heart feels them and your unconscious mind knows they're there.

Please—make a decision *today* to focus on your power. What is *possible*, available, and exciting in life?

Turn the Light On

Maybe you have been living in a dark room for forty years or so, and the last time you felt light and free was when you three or five. At this point, maybe you've stopped even trying to find your way back to bliss.

If this is you, you are going to be amazed at what you will soon discover.

When you wake up tomorrow, I want you to visualize a bright, unfiltered room full of possibility. You will reveal the illusion of obstacle. Starting tomorrow, you will adopt a new mindset, and you will start using new tools. You control what happens in your life, and it's time to build an amazing bridge to the future "new you!"

It's time to turn the light on. This is your new life.

- How will you flip on your switch?

- What will your new life look like tomorrow morning when you wake up?

- What will you feel, think, say, and do with that light?

CHAPTER SIX:
Your New Reality

Reality is not happening to you.
You create reality.

I've already introduced you to some concepts in this book that I believe will rock your world. But, the next few chapters are going to blow your mind. Your entire view of the world is up for grabs.

I want you to get really excited to dive into the "new you." Get ready to really acquire *new* knowledge, *new* technology, and a *new* mindset as we step into your future. You are going to start seeing things in a new light, and this transition will cement the shifts that began as you moved from the "old you."

Remember, though, don't disrespect the "old you." Just like everyone else on this planet, you have done the best you could with the tools you had available in the past.

But now... it's time to climb into your new reality...

The Cliff and the Step-Ladder

Somewhere right now in Western Colorado, there's a woman climbing an 800-foot cliff. It's a challenging cliff and a technical climb. She is hanging from a steep incline and lingering over the edge, strategically maneuvering up the rock. As she looks upward, her heart moves into her throat as she realizes what's coming. Near the very top of the cliff, she must perform a difficult inverted transition in order to reacquire the rock and summit the mountain.

Now, put yourself in her situation. Could you do this? What if the drop were only a few feet off the ground? What if you were only maneuvering over a four-foot wide plank on your driveway? You could probably do a somersault or even a cartwheel from there, right? Most people would have no trouble at all doing jumping jacks from just a few feet off the ground.

It's all a matter of perspective.

The *context* is actually what creates your reality. Neither the four-foot wide plank, nor the steep cliff really matter—it's the context within your own world about what you think is possible that matters. The rock climber balancing off a steep incline has supreme confidence that she will successfully release and reacquire the cliff. She has a vision for what is coming and believes in herself completely. Freeze-frame her in this moment, right before she's ready to make her move.

In that split second, look at her blood and her adrenals. Look at the cortisol levels in her blood and the neural peptides floating through her blood. Put a PET scan on her brain, and let's look inside to see what her neural nets are actually doing.

Everything is fired up, pulsating, and alive inside her.

In contrast, I also want you to do a PET scan of my brain and look inside to see what *my* neural nets are doing as I... put up Christmas lights on an 8-foot ladder. You see, I am scared of heights. Even though I jumped out of a lot of planes during my military career and did a lot of dangerous things on duty, I'm still scared of heights. I can get up on the stepladder, but my knees will be knocking, my stomach will be weak, and frankly, I'll be scared out of my mind up there.

And so, if you looked at my test results in this moment, all my neural nets would also be on fire, pulsating, and fully alive.

So, what's the difference between me and this woman dangling off an 800-foot cliff? Besides our respective realities, there is none. We are both staring in the face of fear and stretching ourselves to the limit.

Our PET scans and blood tests will actually look identical—even though our experiences are vastly different.

Trippy, huh?

Well, here's what's different. At her core, the mountain climber is saying to herself, "I've never been more *alive* than I am right now." She is excited to be charged up and grateful to be in her present position.

Now, a lot of people think that adrenaline junkies flirt with death because of some "death" wish. However, the truth is quite the opposite—they do it because it *highlights life*. For the mountain climber, taking her body to an extreme makes her *feel alive*. Her life, her purpose, her body, her truth, her heart, and her mind has never been more alive than they are in that moment of challenge.

But, back on the eight-foot stepladder, I've never been closer to... death! Inside, my brain is lit up just the same as the mountain climber's, but at the core of my being, I'm thinking, "I'm about to *die*. I am scared to death."

How you perceive a challenge in life is up to your individual perspective. Whether it's the ladder or the cliff that lights up your mind, neither is reality. *You* are your reality. It's not what actually happens; it's what that experience *means* to you that matters.

Let me make this all more personal. When you are facing an economic problem, a relationship problem, or something that deeply upsets you... that *something* is not creating your reality, *you are*.

So, what can you do to change the experience? (Good question.)

Start asking yourself in those pivotal moments, "Am I in the adrenaline of life right now," "Have I never felt more alive," "Am I overflowing with excitement even though I'm doing something incredibly difficult and dangerous?" or "Do I feel closer to death in this moment," "How would I like to feel," "Can I turn my fear into excitement?"

You have the option to create the moments in your life exactly as you want them to be. You're not helpless. You're not a victim in life. You are a creator.

You have the ability to redesign your life, and if you choose, it can be *completely different.* There are no limits!

Let's upgrade your system.

Windows '61

Just like all computers, your brain runs a basic operating system. This computer does a lot amazing of things, however, it can also have many problems. It can suffer from a power surge, the code might get corrupted, and you might have to reboot it from time to time. Occasionally, you may even have to reload the software completely.

Your brain also has functional add-on modules like a spouse, friends, mom, dad, business executive, etc., and you are constantly uploading new add-ons through TV, books, sporting events, and work. Make sense?

Thus, besides your fundamental upgrades and add-ons, the quality of the information you upload directly influences the rest of your program. What books do you read? How much television do you watch? *All of this is uploaded in your system.*

And, what do you do to reboot? Do you go out for lunch with a friend? Pray? Meditate? Talk to your coach or counselor? Or, do you walk away when things get tough?

Then, there are viruses. Do you allow bad data to infiltrate your mind, i.e. criticism? Or, are your internal firewalls set too high? And, are you able to receive good data, i.e. compliments?

This metaphor is endless.

But, here's what's most important—of all the things you can do to ensure quality brain/computer maintenance, this one is critical.

You must keep your operating system updated.

Most people are running systems that are at least two decades—if not five or six decades old. Here's how it works.

First, calculate the year in which you were five years old. Traditional psychology and the latest professionals in neural sciences agree that your personality is fixed by age five. Therefore, at best, you are probably running software from that year. For me, that was 1961.

However, *many* people are running a program that's even *older* than that. Most women are running their mother's program from the year *she* turned five years old, and most men are running the software established by their father when *he* was five years old.

For example, since my dad was five in 1931, unless I do anything to consciously update my "software" (which means not just *improving* my life, but actually reprogramming a new way of looking at things), I will be left trying to succeed in the 21st century running *Windows '61* software installed by a technician with all the default settings of *Windows '31*!

Whether your software is *Windows '65, '75* or *'90*, it doesn't matter. The point is you need to upgrade and rewrite your software to make it current because your reality today does not matter; the software you use to process your reality does.

Think about this—the most successful superstars of our time don't even run software of the current year—they are using future programs like *Windows 2015* or *2025*!

What do you need to do to install a new way of thinking and reboot? Once you've made this upgrade, you'll be ready for another truth...

Discovering Magic

As a society, we often believe that in order to work through a complicated issue, we must work hard and spend a lot of time on a subject.

This seems noble, however, it's simply not true.

Have you ever watched a talented magician like David Copperfield perform a trick and then thought to yourself, "Wow! How did he do that?"

Or, have you ever had a friend perform an impressive card trick and then asked him to show you how it was done?

In both instances, here's what's interesting, once you understand *how* the trick is done, you'll never be fooled by it again. You never have to work to understand the illusion again, no matter how complicated and impossible it initially seemed.

Similarly, after a good teacher explains a new distinction or mindset to you and you "get it," you will be able to grasp similar concepts in a single second. You will never fall back to an old way of being, and you will instantly be able to apply what you've learned.

While the "old you" was busy working to solve a "non-problem," an illusion, the "new you" is ready to understand some life secrets that may seem like magic to you right now.

It's time to create a new cookbook.

Recipes

In my seminars, when I ask most people if they are a good cooks, about 50% raise their hands. I take the bad cooks through an example of how to get a magical, extraordinary recipe for an incredible dessert. Then I ask, "If you follow this recipe, what will you cook?" The sad truth is that most say, "I probably wouldn't follow the recipe" or "I would find a way to screw it up."

How sad is that? The truth is, *if you follow an incredible recipe, you will always create an incredible dessert."*

Right now—you have all the ingredients needed to create everything you want in life—you just need the right recipe to make it happen. And, once you have the recipe, you'll be able to use it forever. It is never the cook who is bad; it is always the recipe.

Whether you know it right now or not, you are already an amazing, magical chef. When you change your cookbook for life and update your software, you will change your strategies, your approach, your patterns, and your emotional triggers.

- Do your challenges make you feel "alive"? Or, do you feel afraid?

- When was the last time you upgraded your software?

- What "operating system" are you currently running?

CHAPTER SEVEN:
Moving Towards Greatness

*Perhaps what you are really afraid of is the light,
and the dark is actually pretty comfortable.*

Now that you're moving towards "Windows 2011," we also need to update the programs you've been running. Just like Word or Excel, you have several "meta-programs" that control how you function each day.

And, one of the most powerful and prolific programs you run is what is called "Towards and Away."

Here's how it works. Your life is in constant motion, and you are always either moving towards what you want or away from what you don't want.

Think about this for a moment, and feel how it applies to your life.

In life overall, are you moving towards what you want, or are you moving away from what you *don't want*? What is your primary psychological driver and source of motivation?

This is the program that creates your reality.

Several studies indicate that less than 10 percent of people operate from a "towards" pattern. These are the individuals who predominantly and consistently produce outcomes and results for themselves by *knowing what they want*. People who come from this place are obsessed with obtaining their end result. Time has no meaning; there are no stipulations. Regardless of how long it takes or what it might take, visualizing and embodying the joy of obtaining their end target is completely worthwhile.

When you *must have* something, there is a direction to your life. You will head towards the thing that you want *no matter what*. Sometimes you will have progress, other times you may get a little stagnant, and you may even get completely stuck from time to time. However, you will *always* continue to move forward. Ultimately, you'll find pleasure in any progress you make because you'll know that you're moving towards what you *really* want in life.

The progress you make while moving towards pleasure will be based on a series of decisions. However, I have another secret to share with you—as long as you're working towards what you really want in life, there are *no wrong decisions*.

Think about this—does anyone ever think, "Hmm. Let's see, here is the right choice, and here is the wrong choice—I think I will do the wrong thing today." Of course not. Here's what happens.

When you are in a "towards" pattern, you're able to see this truth. All decisions are "right"—some are just more right and others are less right. The less right answers don't really bug you too much while in this "towards" mindset though because they always bring you value in the form of a lesson.

Eleanor Roosevelt asked a great question: is failure the opposite of success? Most believe, of course, that it is. She says that it is not. In fact,

Eleanor proclaims that to have success, you *must* have failure, and to have *great success*, you must have *great failure.*

This is one of the best truths about this pattern. Even on your worst day on the planet, when you're in a "towards" pattern, your worst day is only "less pleasure."

How great is that!

This fact is key to your growth towards *The Inevitable You*®. If we measure all of the love, money, joy, and happiness in the planet, the 10 percent of people who are "moving towards" their desires in life have 98 percent of it.

So now, let's talk about the other 90 percent. Here is their primary thought process: "I don't want this problem," "I can't stand this job," "I've had enough of this relationship," "I don't like this place," and "I don't want to be poor any longer."

These people are *not wired to win* because they are consistently stuck in what they "don't want." This group is driven by pain and how to avoid pain. As intensely as "towards-driven" people move towards pleasure, this group obsesses about their pain, and as a result, every day of their life gets worse; every day gets harder. On their very best day, "away-driven" people will only get to experience *less* of what they don't want. They will define success as "less wrong," and they may never even know the feeling of true fulfillment. What is "better" in their life will only be a little less painful.

And, because their focus is about less pain, and pain is always attached to "wrong" decisions, there is a profound sadness amongst this group.

In fact, it physically pains me when I meet clients coming from this place because life doesn't have to be this way. Let me give you an example.

I'd like to introduce you to Dr. A and Dr. B.

Dr. A was 11-years-old when he decided he wanted to become a doctor. As a result of his supreme dedication, he went on to get great grades in high school, college, and med school. He was always at the top of his class and worked very hard towards his dream. He is now a respected doctor in his community.

Would you say that Dr. A is in a "towards" or "away" pattern?) Don't over-think this—it's a metaphor, and the question isn't complicated.) As far as we can tell, he's in a "towards" pattern, right?

In a parallel universe, meet Dr. B. Now, on a superficial basis, Dr. B is identical to Dr. A. He knew he wanted to be a doctor at age 11, he got good grades all through school, and he now owns and operates a successful practice that he loves in his hometown.

Here's the difference.

Dr. A is not just a doctor; he is also a saxophone player. He once picked up a saxophone at a very young age and could play it nearly perfect from the beginning. He was incredible, and he loved playing. However, Dr. A's mom was a doctor, his dad was a doctor, and his grandparents were doctors. They always told him, "Dr. A, when you grow up, you're going to be a doctor because that's what we do. We heal people, we make good money, and we contribute to the community. You're going to be a doctor just like the rest of us."

And so, about the time Dr. A was 11, he was convinced. "Yeah, I probably do want to be a doctor. I don't want to live in smoky bars and have a run-down trailer for a house," he decided.

But, even today, Dr. A still relishes in playing the saxophone. In his spare time, he records music in his private studio and plays in a popular garage band. After all these years, he is *still* a world-class musician.

Now that you know a little bit more about Dr. A, would you still say he is operating from a "towards" pattern? Of course not. He's been moving away from a life of potential poverty and from disappointing his family. If a person grows up thinking, "I'll never be poor, I'll never be poor, I'm never going to be poor," he may be able to create a lot of wealth for himself. But, even if he figures out how to acquire a million dollars, do you think that person is happy, fulfilled, powerful, and loving life?

Absolutely not. Regardless of your success, when you're driven by what you don't want, every decision will ultimately be based on avoiding pain.

Let's go back to Dr. B. When he was 11, Dr. B got very, very sick. He was in and out of hospitals, and his condition grew very dire. His family was prepared to lose him. However, just as they were all about to give up hope, Dr. B went to see a phenomenal doctor who literally saved his life. Dr. B never forgot how important this gift was to him, and he became very passionate about dedicating his life to healing others.

Quite obviously, Dr. B is in a "moving towards" pattern. His practice is set up to satisfy a life-long passion, and his focus has always been moving towards the fulfillment of saving lives.

So, what's the point of this entire story? Sometimes, you can't tell what really drives you until you dig a little deeper. Sometimes you have to look at the foundation behind your psychology to see which path you're on.

One more point on this topic. Once you embody your "towards" pattern, there are three simple rules that, if followed, will guarantee a magical, powerful life.

First of all, if you are moving towards a "must," you will *always* achieve it. It may take a little longer than you thought, and the details may shift, but those changes will probably make the final result even better than you imagined. Accept this. Don't get so tied to the details that you lose sight of the bigger, ultimate vision. Just stay focused and you will get what you want.

Second, know that your "towards" vision may be too large to fit in your lifetime. The man who built Crazy Mountain comes to mind. His vision was huge, and he was able to make a large impact on its completion before his death. Even though he died before it was finished, his legacy lives on through his children who still work on the project to this day. Being in a "towards" pattern is more about the journey than the destination. Even if you don't see a vision through to its finality, you will still feel vibrant, fulfilled, and rewarded while en route.

Lastly, *never stop wanting what you want.* You cannot give up or compromise. Maybe life has beaten you down; maybe you've started to believe you're not really "good enough" to create your true desires. Remember—you are expected to fail on the way to success. The only way you can ever truly fail is to quit, give up, or back away.

This is a powerful formula for success. Start looking at the decisions you're making—are you "moving towards" your goals or are you "moving away" from something?

Greatness only lies at the end of an incredible blueprint that you design for yourself. It is your personal rainbow, your vision, and hopefully, seeing and understanding this tool will allow you to do some deep work moving forward.

How Do Smart People Get Screwed Up?

So, if the difference between pain and pleasure in life is so simple, by now you may be asking, "How did such smart people get so screwed up?"

Remember when I told you that four-year-olds never operate in an "away pattern"? They always focus on what they want. Do you also remember when I told you the story about not "spilling the milk"?

Well, there's more to all of that. Whenever you create something, your brain constantly cycles these three steps. One, you ask several questions. "What does this moment, this breath, and this sequence *mean*," "Is this safe," "Is this dangerous," "Is there too much risk," "Do the means justify the reward," "Am I okay," "Am I safe," "Do I care," "Do I not care," "What does this *mean*?"

Next, once your brain assigns a meaning, and it triggers a corresponding emotional response, you will become happy, sad, angry, ambivalent, engaged, or annoyed as appropriate.

Finally, with the meaning understood and an emotion assigned, you will decide on an action to take. You will decide to act courageously or cowardly, you will move forward with caution, you will leap forward in anticipation, or perhaps you will not act at all (which is also an action).

Thus, all actions start with meaning.

When you assign a negative meaning to a moment, there's very little chance you will take actions that can lead to a positive outcome. You may avoid "failure" and "pain," and you will likely call that success. However, you will limit your true potential. In contrast, when you start with a positive meaning, you will embody positive emotions and take corresponding positive actions. As a result, there is a high probability that starting with a positive meaning will draw you towards positive and fulfilling results.

Bottom line—be conscious of this internal command sequence, and use it to create the reality you desire.

Once again, I can't really overemphasize this counterintuitive point enough—when your chips are down or the planet is storming on you, *that is when this type of awareness is most crucial... and most easily forgotten.* So, be prepared, and don't let yourself fall back when it really matters.

Now, I'm not saying that you should *never* move away from something. The fact of the matter is, it will actually help you spark a change from time to time. Sometimes "moving away" is the catalyst you *need* to start "turning the bus around." What's most important is—how do you feel afterwards? What's your excitement level? Where's your power meter running when you're done talking to yourself through your plan of action?

For example, stopping yourself from watching TV in order to read a book you're excited about is a positive "moving away" pattern. However, there is also an even more empowering way to engage in this internal dialogue.

Suppose you say to yourself, "I've got to stop watching TV so much because I want to start that book on Teddy Roosevelt tonight after the kids go to bed. I'm just excited about that book. I've heard great things about it, and I love the book jacket. Oh, I can't wait to sit down with that book!" This internal conversation is different from, "I've got to stop watching TV, and I'm exhausted."

Can you feel how a positive command sequence issues a different emotional attachment and begins to tap into deeper power and potential for you?

Here's another example. Instead of saying to yourself, "I should swing by the bookstore and buy a diet book," you might choose to say, "Food is not love. Food is fuel; it's energy. I'm going to stop at the grocery store and get some great nutritious food tonight on my way home. I'm also going to pick up a nutrition book because it might have some great distinctions that could help my storehouse of greatness. I love my body. I love the direction in which my life is moving, and I want to be sure I am healthy enough to enjoy it all!   I can't wait to stop at the store!"

Can you feel the difference?

One last thought on this—be sure not to attach judgment to any internal command. The point is to be conscious about the process so that you can choose what's most fulfilling and empowering for you, not to give yourself another reason to beat yourself up.

And so... get ready to depart. You are the captain of the ship! Where would you like to sail?

- What are you focused on?

- What do you believe about yourself?

- Do you have an incredible vision that's driving you? Or, are you motivated by pain?

- Are you trying to get away from something? Or, are you moving towards an empowering future?

CHAPTER EIGHT:
Your Target

Anything that is not growing, is dying.

It's time for a few more layers of power.

Sometime around the first day of a new year, most people take some time to create a few goals. In addition, if you're organized, you may keep a running list of tasks that you need to accomplish each day in order to maintain progress towards those goals. And, if you are one of an elite few, you may actually write down your big-picture goals on a regular basis, as well.

You may also be one of an even more elite group of goal-setters who follow principles such as Stephen Covey's "7 Habits of Highly Effective People." This powerful group believes in being proactive about life. They stay ahead of the curve by trouble-shooting in advance to avoid large challenges and problems while creating their reality *every day*.

There are still other super achievers who believe they can create their *future* reality. These are those savvy planners who create S.M.A.R.T.

(Specific, Measurable, Action-Oriented, Realistic, and Time-Sensitive) goals and keep track of their progress regularly. *Only the top three percent of people live here.*

Can you feel difference in each of these approaches? Can you see how success would be more prevalent in those who incorporate the most goal-setting tactics into their day-to-day life?

That is definitely true. However, there is an even *higher* level that very few people understand.

The *most* successful people in life incorporate their goals into the way they *think* every day.

Whoa. What does that mean?

It all starts with a target.

You see, there is a difference between simply writing down a list of goals and driving towards an integrated target.

Ponder this—if I were to hypnotize you and tell you that there is a rose under your nose while asking you to smell it, focus on it, and think about it, do you think your brain would know whether the rose was really there or not? Of course it would, *and...* of course it wouldn't.

One part of your brain would know you are hypnotized while another part would simultaneously fire the neural nets associated with a real rose. Therefore, at a conscious level, *you* would not know the difference. You would be able to smell the rose exactly as if it were actually there.

Similarly, if you *know* the overall *target* you are aiming towards in life, you can *visualize* the complete experience before you even get there. You can literally put yourself in the situation, engage all five senses in the process, and thereby create an interesting change in your body. *Thinking* your goals prepares you at a deep, unconscious level so that by the time you get there, you've already achieved what you want and know *exactly* what to do.

This, my friend, is where the game of life begins.

A target-driven life gives you the ability to create tomorrow, today.

People in the top one percent of the population create their life targets and move towards them as if they have already happened. By deeply visualizing their success, they bring the future back with them and use that knowledge to take positive, powerful, and decisive actions.

When *you* master this process (and you will) you have the ability to be incredibly magical.

Are you familiar with Roger Bannister's story? It explains how he broke the four-minute mile. Basically, Bannister ran the course over and over and over again in his mind. Each time, he felt the crunch of the cinders under his shoes, he heard the deep sound of his own breath, and he worked against the acid building in his muscles. Each time, he intensely focused on the final stopwatch clicking at 03:59.4 over and over and over again. He lived the race countless times in his mind before he actually completed it, and by the time he ran, it happened *just* as he imagined.

Have you ever done something like this?

If you are like most of my clients, you'll say "no." However, to that response, I say, "Hooey."

Most people do this *every* day—just upside down. Instead of visualizing the future that you *do* want, you likely have been spending time deeply visualizing and emotionally experiencing the future that you *don't* want such as worry, anxiety, and unease.

Don't you think it's time to try visualizing and fully experiencing your deepest desires instead? It's fun! This is one of the greatest tools you own—so put it to use!

Here's another tool I created to help you fully employ this concept.

The Equation of Life

Although many people are deeply inspired and have great intentions after hearing information like this, they also have a very difficult time going back into their life and actually integrating these tools.

Well, here's my solution. I call it the "Equation of Life."

$R = \underline{a} \times (EIM) \times \underline{t}$. This stands for: *Reality = Ask X (Emotional Intensity) X Time.*

Looks complicated, right? Don't worry—it's not. Because I'm an engineer at heart, it was easier for me to express this concept as a formula. However, please don't get turned off by the math. Whether you call it praying, dreaming, or manifesting, the process for effectively connecting the dots between your deepest desire and your actual reality is the same.

So, let me explain what each part means. "R" in this equation is "reality." This is what you create and attract towards yourself.

The "A" in the formula is what you "ask" for. The movie, *The Secret,* did a great job teaching people, "Ask for what you want, not what you don't want." But, I want to expand on this a bit further.

When you ask for what you want, you get a "1" in this equation, and when you ask for what you *don't want,* you get a "-1." Why is the value only "1" either way? Because whether you operate from a New Age, quantum physics, conventional, or biblical system, there is no difference between asking for something big versus asking for something small. The difference is only your request, and you get what you ask for. In very practical and real terms, there's no difference between asking for 1 dollar, 1 million dollars, or a parking space. It's all just energy.

I want you to be able to tap into this river of energy where all of your potential flows. Life is not actually harder or easier—only your mind is limited in what it can create for you. And unfortunately, since most people are too busy focusing on what they don't want, they have no idea what they are missing.

So, here's how to make an energetic request. First, you must embody the emotion you would have if you had achieved your desire in your body. If you're asking for money, you must embody the feelings of prosperity and abundance. If you're asking for a relationship, you must embody love. If you're asking for health, you must embody peace and wellness. Note: When the corresponding emotion is (intensely) present, it will be easier to fully BELIEVE.

Now, some people may try to tell me, "Well, I think that's disingenuous," or "That's faking it until you make it."

If you fall into this category, I'm going to challenge you. In fact, I would wager that if you fall into this category, you are probably among the 90 percent of people who *aren't getting what they really want.* Yet, you probably already employ this principle—in a negative way. You are too busy thinking about the opposite of what you really want to even consider opening your mind.

You'll drive to a sales appointment and think, "I must get this business. If I don't get this sale, I won't be able to make my mortgage payment. I just can't lose this deal."

What type of emotion do you think you have in your body while doing this? And, how intense are your emotions around the experience? If this is how you operate, you also probably take your vision *far* into the future and live in fear and anxiety with the consequences that you *don't want*.

So, since you're already an expert in directing energy to manifest in your life, don't you think that it might be a good idea to try this in reverse?

Think of all the times you've been anxious about an outcome you fear. Can you remember the last time you were overcome with stress and anxiety while envisioning some terrible potential consequence? How often does the bad outcome end up happening? Not very often, huh? Now, some of you may say, "Well, it works—worry keeps bad things from happening. That's why I do it."

That is as nonsensical as believing that as long as you clap your hands, no elephants will come around. Those people clapping, say the same thing to themselves, "See! It's working! No elephants!"

Are you starting to get this?

Your emotions are the catalyst, the lighter fluid, the jet fuel, and the rocket propulsion fluid for creating your desire and manifesting your future. You can choose something destructive like worry, or you can choose something beneficial or empowering like gratitude. It's up to you—what you choose will be the energy that creates your reality.

So, in order to help you track your future trajectory, I created something I call, "EIM," your Emotional Intensity Meter. It is an imaginary box you can place in front of you, and it has a needle that measures the intensity of your emotions from 1 to 10. A high number is an intense emotion; a low number is a low intensity. This is the next part of the equation, and it represents that the higher your emotions, the more powerful your results will be.

Finally, the last element in the equation is "t," which stands for time. This is measured in hours for the purpose of this formula, and its purpose is simple—the longer you focus on something, the more powerful your results.

Here's an example of how it works.

People will tell me, "Bill, I manifested for an hour every day for two months after watching *The Secret*, and it just doesn't work for me."

No. It's not working for you because you're not doing it 24-7. If you want to make this work for you, it cannot just be a temporary novelty; it must be something you embody *every moment*. People who are really good at using this formula even command their dreams to create for them.

Therefore, if you're spending a lot of time watching TV and asking for nothing, guess what the world's going to cook up and deliver to you? Nothing. If you're constantly distracted and wrapped up in other people's problems, guess what you are manifesting? Challenges.

With this very simple equation, we can measure how you drive your reality. Let's put it into practice, shall we?

Many people come into my office and say, "Oh, Bill, I'm working very hard at manifesting. I focus for an hour every morning. I'm working to create incredible wealth and prosperity for myself, but it's just not working."

Here's what I will do in these (very common) situations. I'll put my client in a chair, and I'll ask him to, "manifest exactly like you manifest at home."

Generally people do something like this. They take a deep breath, they kind of close their eyes, and they clear their head. Then, they will sit there silently with a blank look on their face.

How emotionally intense is that?

Nine times out of ten, if you are not able to manifest your desires, it's because you need to raise your vibration by increasing your emotional intensity. Think out loud about your plans. Move around. If you are visual, create a vision board and look at it while you manifest. Play music that inspires you while manifesting. Let yourself *really feel* what you are drawing towards yourself. Think not just of the achievements your desires bring, but consider all the residual benefits and extraneous consequences, as well. The more you can captivate your emotions, the greater your results will be. You need to practice *feeling the emotion*, not just thinking about it. If you see it as something happening to another future version of yourself, you aren't *in it*.

In contrast, here's what most people are really doing when they manifest. They think to themselves, "Oh, that feels so good *over there*. I have a wild amount of money, *over there*. *Over there*, I can see myself writing a check to my favorite charity. All of that feels so good *over there*."

So, let's put all this together. In our example of the blank-looking client— he is moving towards something he wants (1) with an EIM of "2", (a low emotional intensity), and he focused on his desire for 1 hour. Therefore, the formula for his reality would be 1 x 2 x 1 = 2.

Make sense?

Here's another example. Let's say you go into work one day and immediately realize that the warehouse has completely screwed up your most important sale of the quarter. You get very upset. Your cube-mate then notices your distress and asks what's wrong. When you explain your frustration with the warehouse, your cube mate goes, "They screwed me last week, too! Let's go to lunch and talk about how bad they are."

You then spend several hours fixing the problem, briefing your boss, and explaining the error to your customer. It is a very upsetting morning. During lunch, the more you discuss what happened as a result of this gigantic error, the worse the situation gets. You say, "Oh my Gosh! This is a disaster! My boss is mad; the customer is mad. This is terrible."

And, even if you don't get overtly upset, you still might obsess over this problem with "the fist of doom" that just sitting in the pit of your stomach all morning while thinking, "This is a disaster. I can't believe it. I needed this order to make my mortgage payment this month. I am doomed."

At this point, what do you think your EIM is?

Yes—it's incredibly high.

And, how do you think this affects your reality? You've been moving away from your desires with an emotional intensity of at least eight for about six hours. That's $(-1) \times 8 \times 6 = (-48)$!

Here's what you could have done. You could have come into the office, feeling great because you just spent an hour manifesting abundance. Then, when you opened your email, you could have been thinking, "I'm feeling great. I wonder how that order went."

When you read the news they screwed up, you could think to yourself, "Huh, this is a huge disaster. Hmm. That's bad."

Then, because you're not reacting out loud or causing a commotion, your cube mate doesn't have any idea that you're in distress, which is *huge*. There is now no need to go to lunch and to intensely discuss the problem. Although you do still have to deal with the problem, your boss, and your client, you are now able to do so in a much more positive way because you are not *choosing to feel upset.*

Here's your formula now. After four hours of working on the problem and *not* going to lunch to complain, you're still moving away from something because you're focused on the problem. Your emotional intensity is much lower, and you've spent significantly less time thinking about it. Your formula is now (-1) x 2 x 4 = (-8). By making just a few simple changes, you've increased your vibration six-fold. And, in doing so, you've massively decreased the pain you draw towards yourself.

Are you following me with this?

Now, to merely balance out disaster in your life, you *must* intensely feel your joy when you manifest it. Those clients who don't sit there blankly and who don't put joy *over there* jump out of their chair with excitement. They pace and they exaggerate body gestures. If you would have done that in the morning of your work predicament, your equation for life would look like this: 1 (your ask) X 8 (high EIM) X 1 (the hour you meditated) = 8. You would have just balanced out your warehouse disaster before even stepping foot in the office!

Here's the last piece. If you really want to be a master, here's what you would have done after opening up your email with the bad news about the order. First you would think to yourself, "Oh my gosh, what a huge disaster going on in the warehouse! I can't believe it. I wonder what they did. This is going to be a huge opportunity for me. The customer is going to get to see me fix this problem and so is my boss. I'm going to be a hero today. I can't wait to fix this. This disaster is custom-made for me because I'm a superstar!"

This mindset flips your -1 to a +1, and in this scenario, your focus is on what you are moving towards because you've turned the negative into a positive. Let's say your emotional intensity is at least a six, and you will have to spend about four hours fixing the problem. Thus, your reality will be: 1 x 6 x 4 = 24!

You have now gone from a world of (-48), to a (-8 + 8), to a (24 + 8) by merely utilizing your emotions differently.

Making sense? This is *so* powerful once you understand it. You have the ability to literally transform your reality depending on how you direct your thoughts and corresponding emotions.

Once you start to employ this skill, you're going to discover that your ability to access your own power and to create results is off the hook...

- What's your ultimate target?

- What has been your past EIM?

- Knowing what you now know, how sure are you that you have the capacity to create all that you desire?

CHAPTER NINE:
Self-Imposed Chaos

When you target "good" and fail, you get less. When you target "above average" and fail, you get less. If you fail at being magical, you always get magical results.

As your awareness and power continues to grow, you create a large array of new choices. By now, I hope that you have incorporated at least some of this information into your life and resolved to make some important changes in the way you think and operate. And, even if you are a major over-achiever, there are probably still at least a few places where you're falling back. There are likely a couple areas where your buttons are still getting pressed.

The key to overcoming those situations is balance. You are going to have to let go of your all-black or all-white viewpoints in order to make further on-going progress. From now on, you must seek balance amidst self-imposed chaos and reason amidst emotionally-charged situations.

Let me give you an example so that you can better understand what I'm describing.

Let's look at one of the biggest button-pushers in existence—arguments. What is your consciousness level during an argument? Are you open-minded, level-headed, and operating with lucid clarity? Probably not. If you are invested in your own viewpoint and busy trying to persuade another to see your side, it is virtually impossible to maintain a balanced, fair composure. Even if you are 90 percent right (or even 100), the act of trying to convince someone to see your view requires an enormous amount of energy.

Therefore, in the face of an argument, the best response is to utilize the art of an Aikido master—bring someone around to see your side by creating alignment first. Look for the areas that you agree upon, then discuss your area of disagreement and ask for small shifts. Or, if you can't create alliance on *any* issues, simply agree to disagree. The energy you would otherwise expend during an argument is simply not worth it. That charge is better spent working towards your own fulfillment. Why waste it on miscellaneous little triggers that get you fired up? Practice stepping back, observing the situation, and then making a proactive, empowering choice. The more you do this, the easier it will be (even in the heat of the moment), and the better you will feel when all is said and done.

The same applies to internal arguments. This is when you mess up and beat yourself up repetitively afterwards. You tell yourself, "Oh, I really screwed this up. I'm a terrible person. I can't stand that I failed."

In reality, any screw-up is never that black and white. Again, you must look for alignment within yourself to find the truth of the situation. Did you really get *all* of the experience wrong? Or, was it just a small part? In almost all situations, you probably got most of it right, and it was only a very small error that resulted in a bad end result.

I know all of this is easier said than done. I know it's tough when you're under fire, feeling the heat of your mistakes, or upset about your current life situations.

So, here's a tool to help you during those intense trigger moments.

Living at "Level 10"

Instead of thoughtlessly responding to situations, start asking yourself to rate your reactive consciousness on a scale of 1 to 10. Ask yourself, "On a scale of 1 to 10, what is the power I'm creating with this thought? Is this thinking helping or hurting my reality?"

Once you become well-practiced in this technique and you start to regularly calibrate your thoughts, you'll be able to quickly realize when you're in a "Level 10 Pattern" and when you're moving backwards. It will be very obvious. Plus, after you're able to identify your personal trigger points, you'll also be able to develop resistance measures to counter your hot buttons ahead of time.

As a result, you'll be able to start enjoying life at "Level 10."

Now, living *completely* at a "Level 10" *every day* may feel daunting. It probably even sounds overwhelming and hard. But, here's another interesting counterintuitive truth.

When you live at Level 10, you return to The Inevitable You®, and you already possess this power at a very deep and authentic level.

Remember today what you knew when you were four years old. At that time, everybody is Superman and Superwoman. Everything is a ten.

Four-year-olds play at a ten, laugh at a ten, and cry at a ten, and most importantly—they also sleep at a ten. They don't fester and worry about what happened each day. They don't fret about what tomorrow will bring. They enjoy each moment exactly for what it is. Period.

Living life at a "Level 10" means you have Level 10 thoughts, Level 10 emotions, and Level 10 language—everything's at a 10! When you strive to come from this place every day, life actually becomes *easier*. It's simple and completely authentic. You don't have to go back and redo things. You don't have to calculate contingency plans because you know that you're already amazing and magical. You can simply focus on blowing the planet away with your capabilities.

So, make Level 10 mistakes! Have Level 10 fears! Then... sleep at Level 10, relax at a Level 10, and let it all go. Simply be authentic. This will make your stress feel different, and your anxiety will begin to dissipate. Trust me—living at a Level 10 is much easier than what you're doing now. This is the place where everything opens up to you.

Here's what might get in your way.

Fear & Failure in Tandem

While all of the tools I've shared with you in this book so far are intertwined, fear and failure are unique in how they cycle with one another. What that means is, as one is impacted, so is the other, but not in the way you may think.

Most people believe that as fear increases, so does failure. This seems to make sense, right? However, *the opposite is actually true*. As your fear increases, your adrenals kick in and boost your energy. Your thoughts become clearer, and your actions become more precise when you're under pressure. As a result, operating under fear actually *decreases* failure.

However, since most people don't understand the benefits of fear, they simply stop trying once they get scared. As the risk goes up, so does avoidance. You can come up with hundreds of ways to protect yourself from all potential pain, but what you are really doing is turning your hope into stagnant, yet pragmatic realism. What you are really doing is giving up before you even get started.

Ironically, when your fear decreases, your potential for failure increases. When you're not in fear, you're one of three things—cocky, comfortable, or apathetic, all of which make you more prone to mistakes. Plus, when you're not in fear, you don't benefit from an adrenal rush and the heightened senses that go with it.

On the other hand, if you look at how failure influences fear, the pattern is more intuitive. As failure increases, so does fear. As failure decreases, fear dissipates. Make sense?

This is what I want you to understand—failure leads to fear, not the other way around. It's crucial for you to understand this distinction because fear has likely been at least one of the excuses holding you back up until this point. Now it's time to let fear go. When you separate fear from failure, it's clear that fear is *just an excuse.* It's not a valid reason to avoid taking the risks that will bring you fulfillment.

I'm excited for you!

As the "new you" begins to apply this notion, you're going to discover an entirely new vantage point. You'll be able to see fear as a friend to keep you sharp, and you're going to be able to clearly see how your "old you" perspective has held you back.

For the "new you," fear is not only something to embrace, it's something to celebrate. Think about it. As a fear rises, you're able to climb to a new part of the mountain you've never been on before. You're no longer idle where the "old you" was stuck. You're dealing with higher expectations and higher standards for yourself. And, as a result, you're going to get to experience the world in a whole new way.

Now that you are creating your "new you" reality, I'm going to ask you to evolve *even more*. You must not only see failure as beneficial, but you must see it as a mandatory and crucial ingredient on the road to your ultimate success. I want you to fully appreciate the concept that *failure actually leads to joy*.

And, the greater the success you shoot for, the greater your failure must be to get there. The greater the stakes; the greater the joy.

So, go ahead and make your failures joyous *right now*. Failure is your best friend.

Remember Picabo Street? When she won the gold medal in women's downhill skiing, do you think she did so without failing along the way? No way. She's fallen down the mountain more than anyone else. And, they weren't light, soft falls either. Picabo has had to experience some of the worst bone-breaking, ligament-ripping, and skin-suit shredding worst falls of anyone in order to grow to where she is now.

In contrast, think about all those people who ski blue runs down the mountain every day. They go in for the night, settle into a hot-tub with a cold beer, and brag to all their friends, "Hey guys, I had a great day. *I didn't even fall once*."

Maybe they had an enjoyable, comfortable day, but it wasn't *exhilarating* and deeply fulfilling. Those blue run skiers didn't fall, but they didn't stretch or improve all day either.

I can hear some of you shuddering at this point. This concept is another counterintuitive phenomenon. To be clear, I'm not saying that you must fail to get everything you want in life. It's just that you must fail when stretching beyond your comfort zone. The harder something seems to you right now, the more you must fail to achieve it, but the more rewarding it will then be, as well.

So, let's wire this all in.

If you have been operating with a failure-avoidance focus, you've probably been in a stagnant, unfulfilled, and boring place. You've been busy doing *nothing*.

And, if you've been operating from a fear-avoidance focus, you've probably been paralyzed in a state of constant stress and anxiety.

Either way, you've been stuck, which is okay for now. And, if all of this isn't resonating with you yet, that's okay, too. It can be complicated and somewhat overwhelming to take it all in at first. Just take a deep breath. You've actually come much farther than you realize. Could the "old you" have even put "failure" and "joy" in the same sentence?

Fear and failure in tandem has kept so many people down for so long. You can't just tell yourself to be fearless on cue. Not only is that virtually impossible, it's also nonsensical.

And so, if you take absolutely nothing else out of this chapter, here's the crucial bottom line—whatever you do, don't let fear stop you from moving forward towards your dreams. Instead, when your fear increases, rejoice in it, celebrate a new impending breakthrough, and use your heightened awareness to your advantage.

Congratulations on how far you've come…

- Are you prepared to commit to a Level 10? Why or why not?

- What are your personal hot buttons? How can you find balance in those situations to see the full, big picture?

- What old fears have haunted you the most?

- What old failures have haunted you the most?

- What are you going to do differently tomorrow to release your illusion of obstacles?

CHAPTER TEN:
Your Emotional Quotient

Make your fears smaller and your greatness greater.

Wow, are you as excited as I am? I hope so. Your excitement should be tinged with both apprehension and anxiety. It's simultaneously half full and half empty, right? Now you get that, right? Good.

You have shifted from the "old you," to a new reality, and to an entirely new level of consciousness. Now, I want you to return back to the consciousness and awareness of that four-year-old you once again. Your knowledge was less then, but your consciousness was greater. The old expression, "If I only knew then what I know now...," has two problems.

First, it's demeaning. In saying this, you imply that if you were better then, you would be better now. Well that's hooey, isn't it? Especially in light of your growth and evolution through this book.

Second, you now know the four-year-old inside you is authentic in a way you have forgotten. Therefore, here's a better expression, "I command to remember now what I knew then."

So, here is a tool to help you reinforce that natural, free, and innate state of being.

Your Emotional Quotient

At the beginning of this section, we talked about how emotions ultimately drive the reality you're experiencing right now, we talked about how to re-frame the meaning you give experiences, and we talked about how to use this level of consciousness when you encounter problems. Although you will still encounter all the same problems others do, you now have a much better approach. When everybody else reacts to and struggles with reality, you will say "I *want* this to be my truth, I *want* this to happen. I command my potential to create this truth for me. I want more of this."

Being able to manage your focus, your experiential meanings, and the emotions that you create is *unbelievably powerful*.

In fact, a great author, Daniel Goleman, described emotions in an especially interesting way. After compounding about two decades of research into a thorough body of work, he coined the term, "emotional quotient" or "EQ."

Here's the premise of his work. Basically, our society has measured our potential for success on an "IQ" or "Intellectual Quotient" Score for several decades. We've consistently placed those with a high IQ on a pedestal and believed that high intelligence will lead to equally high life rewards. However, in contrast, Goleman's theory proves that a person's EQ can actually more accurately predict success.

If you really think about it, this makes sense. We've all seen some really, really smart people who didn't have the common sense to get out of a wet paper bag. And, we've all seen other people, who, though not as intellectually gifted, achieve great heights.

So, even though we've known a high IQ doesn't necessarily drive success, most of us have allowed the label to control many of our life decisions. We hang onto IQ as the main driver in life. If someone once told you your IQ was high, you probably accepted it as a gift and applied that meaning in one way or another. In contrast, if someone once told you that your IQ was low, you probably never felt very smart growing up.

When Goleman introduced his EQ research, he changed this standard. Here's what he discovered.

When he looked at the average CEO in America, he found that their IQ was higher than their EQ as traditionally accepted. *However*, when he tested the superstar, over-achiever, top CEOs, the reverse was true. Their EQ was consistently higher then their IQ. As a result, of his findings, Goleman theorized that having a high EQ is the "it" factor that makes some people wired for the highest echelon of success. It is the difference between good and exceptional leaders. He concluded that EQ is what gives someone the ability to inspire, motivate, and emotionally connect with others.

For those intellectuals reading this book, you may be saying to yourself, "I want to follow the leader who is *right*, not just the one who makes me feel good."

Well, here is the deeper truth. Your EQ is also the willpower that pushes you through obstacles. A leader with a high EQ solves problems better and faster, and he intuitively knows how to use the entire team's synergy to benefit the company. Plus, because he will not be dragged into any unnecessary drama, he is able to maintain the clear mind needed to make better, "right" decisions.

Are you getting how powerful your emotions are? Your ability to emotionalize by consciously associating and disassociating to your life experiences is _the key_. Managing your emotions is the core message behind *The Secret,* and it's the driving force behind all other aspects of personal development, as well.

But, unfortunately, emotions have been trained out of you over the years. Again, would a four-year-old have this problem? All four-year-olds have great fluency in emotionality. They are gifted in reading, understanding, using, and expressing a large spectrum of emotions without guile. They live organically, honestly, and without manipulation.

If you can tap back into this ability as an adult, not only will it feel good, it will enhance your ability to find fulfillment ten-fold.

Because at the end of the day, it doesn't really matter how much wealth and success you acquire, what matters is how you *feel* about it. What matters is your EQ. Even if you are the biggest loser on the planet, if you have a high EQ, you're going to feel good, and people love people who feel good. They are those we want to be around.

All that said, this may be easier said than done. A lot of what I have taught you up to this point is fairly straightforward. However, this one requires some art and pizzazz. If you aren't emotional to begin with (which a good percentage of my clients aren't), this is going to feel like a foreign language to you, and I get that. Please REMEMBER WHO YOU WERE—this wasn't a foreign language to you at age four. You have this knowledge somewhere deep inside you.

Use your "new you" awareness. Design yourself as who you would like to be today, and use your emotions to get there. I promise it will only feel strange for a little while.

- What is your current EQ?

- How can you strengthen your EQ attributes?

CHAPTER ELEVEN:
Power Questions
(lead to the Inevitable® Question)

Know what you want,
and know what you don't want.

I'm about to introduce you to some more amazing tools in the next few chapters. These tools are "the bomb." They are insanely powerful and amazing. But, you've got to embrace them as the "new you." You've got to fight through the fear and failure tandem that's going to try to sabotage you.

Are you with me?

First... I'd like to rock your world by explaining the power of questions.

Now, as we've already established, our brains work very much like a computer. We are wired to cue questions, to seek answers, and to logically process our experiences. Just like a computer program, we constantly ask ourselves a series of questions and sub-questions until we eventually drill down and settle on a defined answer that makes sense.

"What do I do with this data," "What should I do with this moment," "What should I focus on," "What does this mean to me," and "What do I think about this?"

Just stop and think about it. Did you just ask yourself a question while thinking about this? You will realize you ask questions _all the time_, across many contexts and in many different ways. Your questions can be resourceful and empowering, or they can be defeating, degrading, and unproductive. Some people consistently ask negative questions even when things are going great, and some people ask positive questions even in the face of challenges. But unfortunately, negative questions are much more common. People usually ask them for one of two reasons.

In a futile effort to protect themselves from some unknown potential event, many people will say to themselves during great times, "What's going to happen to mess all this up?" Then, their brain _will_ answer by seeking out the "what" that will mess up the circumstances.

Can you see how destructive this question can be?

Similarly, other people can enjoy the moment, but close down as soon as a storm rages. As soon as things get rough, their thoughts then turn into negative questions like, "Why am I not good enough," "What's wrong with me," and "Why does this always happen to me?"

If you ask a bad question, you'll get a bad answer.

Being mindful about the questions you ask yourself is _the most important way_ to shift your focus and your life. Remember—_regardless of what you ask, your brain will work to find you an answer._ And, for most people, there is at least one question you ask repeatedly every day. It is your constant focal point and number one internal priority in life. The problem is—this question has become so ingrained in your psyche that it probably isn't even initially clear what it is.

Let's find out. Simply, ask yourself, "What question do I ask myself most consistently," "What question do I ask when I really need to move forward in life," and "What question do I typically ask when I'm under fire and facing something difficult?"

Here are some samples...

"Why do I always find myself in these jams?"

"What do I do to always attract such trouble?"

"Why can't I ever succeed?"

"What am I going to do when "x" happens?"

"Why me?"

"How can I make my life perfect?"

"What's wrong with me?"

Once you've identified your top question, ask yourself, "Where did this question come from? Was it part of your parents' or grandparents' blueprint? Did you learn it at some big failure point in high school or college? What circumstances brought it into my life? What made it even stronger?"

Evaluate whether this question has been helping or hindering you by looking at its overall vibration. Ask yourself, "What do I create when I ask this question? What energy do I generate when asking myself this question?"

Remember, ALL results begin with a thought. No matter what your religious, scientific, or philosophical beliefs are, you create your reality today. Life is not happening to you. Think about this as you ask yourself,

"What am I really creating with these questions? What am I attracting? What am I manifesting into reality?"

Then ask yourself, "What *can't* happen when I ask this question? How will this question hold me back?"

Remember that your "old you" designed this question as a way to protect you. It was not designed with mal-intent, and it was not meant to mislead you. In fact, it was created to support you in a very important way. Therefore, ask yourself, "What's the positive intention behind this question?"

By digging out the positive benefit behind the question you've been asking, you'll be able to maintain positive intent at a higher level, and this will give you the power to design something that can truly serve you— even when your chips are down.

Take a moment, now, to daydream. If you could imagine the most unbelievably powerful life you could lead, what questions would you ask (on a daily basis) to maintain that incredible life? How could you set yourself up to win no matter what? What questions would make you feel fulfilled, excited, passionate, and amazingly resourceful every day? What questions would increase your vibration, enhance your energy, and help you give all experiences empowering meanings?

Here are some positive examples...

"How can I appreciate life even more in this moment?"

"What is the best thing I can do right now to support myself and others?"

"What lesson am I supposed to be learning right now?"

"How can I use this experience to serve the greater good for myself and others?"

As a side note, if your old questions focused on pleasing other people, remove yourself from their chaos *right now.* Remember other peoples' opinions are none of your business anyway—*it's their opinion.* Worrying about what other people think just creates unnecessary feelings of lack, self-loathing, and insecurity. Allow me to use myself as an example.

When I put myself through a similar exercise designed by Tony Robbins about a decade ago, I had a very powerful experience. To fully appreciate the impact this exercise had on my life, you have to understand the context of my life at this stage. I was a very successful executive, I was successful in corporate life, and I had started several companies at various stages in my life. By anyone's measures, I was doing very, very well. And, I was a happy guy for the most part.

But, Tony asked me to identify just *one "primary question"* that really drove my life, and when I thought about it, I realized that in certain situations, particularly in tough cold-calling sales environments, I felt completely disempowered. During these more challenging parts of life, I discovered that I asked myself, "What should I not say, or not do, in order to ensure people won't dislike me?"

Initially, I had no idea where this idea came from. So, I dug deeper and in doing so, I realized something had happened to me in fourth grade that changed my view of the world. Up until fourth grade, I was popular and had a lot of friends, but during that school year, my family chose to move away and I ended up in a new school. And, somehow this unstable transition made me feel embarrassed. I had what I thought was a "mark of shame" on me. I knew if someone got to know me they would like me, but I had to get them to see past this "shame" in order for them to find the "likeable me." So I couldn't ever screw up an initial meeting!

Now, think about the question I was asking, *"What should I not say, or not do, in order to ensure people don't dislike me?"*

First of all, it's a tortured question from the start. How could I *ever* successfully answer that? When I was able to see this disconnect and understood what was really driving me, my entire life changed.

Discovering *The Inevitable You®* is not about therapy; it's not about potty training and making you feel better—it's about discovering the programs, meanings, truths, and patterns that run your life. You have to dig to discover what's behind your motives and then determine what's really serving you and what isn't.

So, here's the question I designed that I now ask myself on a regular basis, *"Every person I meet has an extraordinary story, and it's my job to figure it out—so, what gift will be waiting at the end of that process?"*

Think about that question. Can you see how much more empowering it is? How do you think it affects my ability to make cold calls and to meet new people? I'm now magical at cold calling; it's *easy* for me. It's not because I'm smarter, better, or bigger than I was before; it's because I changed the questions I ask myself.

You can also consciously change and reprogram the questions you use in your life. You can create questions that serve you in absolutely *any* scenario.

I guarantee this will change your life.

You can wake up tomorrow and experience a completely new day.

It's not just the first question you ask that creates reality for you. In fact, there are succeeding layers of questions that drive reality. Whether you are evolved or stuck, if you're asking garbage questions today, you're going to get garbage answers. It's a law—you can't get great answers from terrible questions. So you must dig deep enough to find that one question that will plug your growth. Have you ever played Jenga, the game where you stack logs and pull them out one by one until the tower crumbles? Poor questions are like that, too, only in reverse. They will teeter and wobble, and you will feel unsafe. However, when you pull the right Inevitable® Question from the tower, the illusions holding you back will tumble, and the true new growth, and success can be yours.

You must ask yourself great questions, and your mind will serve you every time. *You will get different results when you ask a different question.*

- What "old you" questions have you been asking?

- What one question is holding you back?

- What new Inevitable® Question will you design to replace it?

- What other, great new questions will serve the "new you"?

CHAPTER TWELVE:
Quantum Reframing

*Your potential is proportionally larger
than your most challenging problem.*

This next tool has a big, fancy, scientific sounding name—"Quantum Reframing."

Sounds complicated, doesn't it?

Well, you already know about reframing. I've mentioned it previously in a number of forms and contexts. It's the way that you choose to perceive the world around you. It's the notion that life can simultaneously be both full and empty, that experiences can be both good and bad, that challenges can be both exhilarating and scary, and that an idea can have both a positive and dangerous value to you. This fine line is the precipice upon which your whole life balances.

The quantum part of this title refers to your *unconscious* decision to define which angle to take. It is the *meaning* that you automatically defer to. The "old you" may have given you black and white options from which to choose, such as, "Is what I just learned good or bad," and "Is this safe or is it dangerous?"

However, the "new you" is always looking for *both* sides. The "new you" asks, "Which side of the coin do I now want? Which way of looking at this situation will serve myself and others?"

Although the full side is highly compelling, you also have to be aware at times of what's empty. You need to be real about the entire picture. Understanding the empty side of things will help you appreciate the complete value of what's full. Taking a holistic approach illuminates the entire situation because sometimes, the shadows can tell us more about the light than the light itself, and sometimes the light is contrasted by the shadow.

Again, this book is not "feel good," pop psychology. The point of becoming *The Inevitable You*® is not to pretend, "Oh, everything is rosy," all the time. It's about deeply understanding every dimension so you can make powerful decisions to create the reality in which you choose to live.

Let's dig deeper on this.

You may have heard that in relationships, the very thing that attracted you to a person is the very thing that is going to drive you most crazy about them. This is their "shadow side."

For example, I have a very powerful wife. I absolutely needed a powerful woman, wanted a powerful woman, and fell in love with this woman instantly when I met her. She is a magnanimous, powerful force of nature with a large personality I love. *And...* she can also be controlling, pushy, and opinionated. She can also drive me crazy. These are two sides of the same coin. The very same character trait that makes me adore this woman is what can also push my buttons.

Are you with me so far?

Let's go even deeper. Procrastination is a great example of quantum reframing. Virtually everybody who comes to my office will say, "Oh, I'm a procrastinator. That's why I can't move forward."

To which I'll respond, "Oh, cool!"

This usually throws them off a bit, and they'll say, "Yeah, well that's a real problem." Then, here's how the rest of the conversation goes:

Me: "Is it? Let's look at it. Are you good at procrastination?"

Client: "Yeah."

Me: "Are you great at procrastination?"

Client: "Yeah."

Me: "Are you a professional procrastinator? Can you procrastinate on anything?"

Client: "Yep. I'm unbelievable, I procrastinate, blah, blah, blah... I'm a professional at procrastinating."

Me: "Great—because you are now going to use this incredible tool to your advantage. You're going to procrastinate on reaching for a Twinkie. You're going to procrastinate on turning on the TV for the entire week! Since you're such a professional at procrastinating, this should be easy for you."

If, like many of my clients, you've been waiting for years to do something different with your life, but haven't because you say that you're a procrastinator, you simply need to use this tool in a new way. Procrastinate in a way that will serve you. If the half-empty side of procrastination is to not do what's good for you, what's the half-full value of procrastination? It's not doing *what's bad for you*. If you can be a pro on one side of the coin, you can apply the same technique to the other side, as well, right?

 To further my point about the *benefit* of procrastination, I'd like to tell you about a scientific study that began at an Ivy League school in the mid-1950s. The focus was on five-year-olds who are now in their 60's, and it proved that one of the factors that most affects success later in life is not intelligence, persistence, appearance, or anything else you might guess. The number one trait that affects a child's later success is his ability to control... delayed gratification.

Here's how they performed the test.

Each of the kids knew he was in a study, but he didn't know its purpose. So, as each came into a room, a scientist offered him a chocolate chip cookie. The scientist would say, "Hey, I need to leave the room for a little bit. You can have this cookie anytime you want while I'm gone. However, if you wait until I come back, I'll give you *two* cookies."

The researchers filmed these kids alone with the cookie in the room (which made for hilarious footage, by the way). A kid would look at the cookie, study the cookie, smell it, taste it, and even put their tongue to it. Some kids ate it right away—they had no ability to delay their gratification. Other kids waited for a very long time, ate a little nibble, then had a few more nibbles, and then finally just ate the entire thing. But, the children who could wait for enormous lengths of time until the scientist came back were few, and these were the kids who ended up being the most successful later in life. As promised, each of these patient kids received two cookies, and in the process, they learned a very valuable lesson that reinforced their dedication to strong will power—delayed gratification results in even more value.

Delayed gratification is the "half-full" side of procrastination.

Here are some other examples...

When I use the expression "light and dark" or "good and bad," most people go "Oh, well that's not even quantum re-framing." But, let's explore this more. We tend to think of things that are light as good and things that are dark as bad. We think good is light and that evil is darkness, and we have a very sharply defined boundary about what is light and what is dark. So, let me ask you a question. What do you think of the words hedonist or gluttonous versus naughty?

When you think of hedonism and gluttony, you go "Oh, those are bad things," right?

But, aren't those really just the darker side of the light spectrum? They describe a level of consumption well beyond moderation. Too much light isn't actually a good thing, is it? Too much darkness is definitely a bad thing, but is a little bit of darkness still bad? Being ornery or naughty is fun, isn't it? There's a little bit of Mae West in all of us. We all laughed when she said, "When I'm good, I'm bad, and when I'm bad, I'm better." A little bit of bad can be good. There are two sides to every coin. The glass is always both half empty *and* half full.

So, the question then becomes, do you have enough consciousness to quantumly re-frame issues to see all sides and to find a view that will serve you? Can you make distinctions between what makes something both half full and half empty and then scale that something to find balance at a deeper level?

If so—this is huge! Understanding how to make this shift significantly raises your EQ, it puts you in the driver's seat of life, and it gives you the inherent ability to be your authentic, four-year-old self.

Let's keep going. This is such a critical concept—I want to give you a lot of examples so that you can really dig into it.

If I told you pain was bad, would you say "Ah yeah, pain is bad. That's a half empty thing. If I'm in pain, that's obviously not a good thing, correct?"

Yes, you are right. But yes, I am also setting you up.

Pain can also be half full. We all love the expression, "No pain, no gain," right? What about the expression, "That which does not kill me, makes me stronger?" Same concept. The Marines used that phrase in a TV commercial not too long ago as a way to attract young men to enlist. Pain can be both good and bad.

Let's continue. Here's another one for you—persistence. That's a great word isn't it? I have clients who come in and tell me, "Oh, Bill I'm so persistent. I never quit until I get what I want. I'm persistent, I have focus, and I am driven. I make things happen."

I'll respond, "Okay, great. That doesn't seem to be a problem. So, why are you here?"

To which they'll say, "Well, I really just don't know when to quit. I constantly push my limits and am constantly overstepping my boundaries."

Hmmm. So, what they're telling me is their greatest strength is also their greatest weakness.

Understanding and applying this concept of quantum reframing is one of my greatest strengths in working with clients. I use this tool all the time to learn more about what's really holding someone back. Because our strengths can be so closely related to our limitations and struggles, it's easy to overlook where they overlap. However, it's absolutely critical to look beneath the surface to see this connection.

Not too long ago, a woman stood up in one of my seminars who claimed there was absolutely *no half full side* to her life. She said that she and her ex-husband were constantly fighting one another over their young daughter. She said that she had spent every last cent trying to keep her ex-husband away but her daughter still wasn't safe. The courts weren't getting it, she was exhausted, and she cried out loud as she worried about the fate of her daughter. "Tell me," she said, "How is all that a positive? What great meaning can I pull from *that!*"

At this point, you could hear a pin drop in the room. The pressure was on.

I asked her, "What do you think it will mean to your daughter 20 years from now when you can tell her with this same Level 10 emotional intensity that you loved her so much you fought for her against all odds and that you spent every last cent you had to make her safe because that is *who you are*? What do you think that level of selflessness, commitment, and love will mean to her?"

With this, the woman began to cry. She just stood there with tears streaming down her face, but a small, little smile began to grow across her face.

You see, it really is *always* true. The glass is always, always, *ALWAYS* both full and empty. It is only your perspective that matters. Know that and no matter how tough it gets or how deeply imbedded in an issue or "truth" you become, *know you can always discover another side*. With all the tools and new awareness we are working on, you have all the tools you need at this point to shift your viewpoint and to see the other side. You may have been defined by your diagnosis, trauma, or "limp" for so long that it will be challenging to walk normal all of a sudden and to have no-one, no-thing, or no-problem to blame. This is the truth, *and* this realization is *more* than worth it. When you emotionalize the "new you," dissociate from the "old you," and commit to a new reality, life becomes *so* sweet. Your history hasn't changed. Your life hasn't changed. Your current problems are still your current problems. But, *you* have changed.

How do you feel now that you have the ability to fully see both sides of the coin? What is it like to really see your life with new eyes?

At the turn of the last century, Marcel Proust had a really great observation. Back then, explorers were the Michael Jordan's of the world. They were the cream of society and adorned as heroes. But, paraphrasing Marcel, he wrote that the real voyage of discovery consists not in seeking new land, but in seeing old lands with new eyes.

As an explorer on this path, <u>you</u> are a hero! And, your new landscape awaits you.

- Where are you currently in your ability to master your emotions? Rate your current EQ on a scale of 1 to 10.

- What can you do to bring your EQ up to a Level 10?

- Pick a challenge that is currently "unsolvable." Reframe all quadrants of the issue, the reality. What did you discover?

CHAPTER THIRTEEN:
Power Thoughts

Emotionalize your successes;
intellectualize your failures.

This next tool is called "Association and Disassociation."

You saw a version of it earlier when I explained "Towards and Away," and it was an essential part of the "Formula for Life." But now, the "new you" can learn to apply this concept by consciously creating your reality and emotionally associating to the excitement each new day brings.

As you continue to dig even deeper into your quantum nature, you will discover a curious fact. Sometimes when you consciously re-frame new emotions to an experience, it feels mismatched and incongruent. This is normal, and this chapter is all about embodying your emotions at a much deeper level.

Here's what you have to do. Once the re-frame takes place, associate or disassociate your emotions accordingly to distance you from those feelings you want or don't want. Ask yourself, "What emotions am I going to associate or disassociate in this time frame, in this instance, moment, or memory? Really look at the experience. What *was* it? What *is* it? What does it *mean*? What do you want to *take from it*?

For example, perhaps in your past, you've been "disassociated" from your greatness. You used to think, "Well, ah shucks, I'm not going to claim my greatness because that would be arrogance. That would be prideful and boastful. I don't want to do that. I'm a humble, humility-based person. I mean, I did win the Nobel Prize last week, but that was nothing. Really, I just got lucky."

I know this is an extreme example, but do you catch my drift?

Our unconscious drive to dissociate from positive and powerful emotions diffuses our innate strength. It mocks our greatness, and makes it *that* much harder to achieve more. Don't just dismiss your power! *Embrace it always.*

By the same token, disassociate from all those things that dis-empower you. Unconsciously, we've been taught it's okay to be depressed, miserable, and half empty. But, it's not okay. *You have a choice.* When you intellectually look at both the half full and half empty sides of life, you're going to choose a meaning you will reinforce as truth.

If you've been living in a "dark" room "broken" for 40 years, you can choose to fully associate to that pain and hang onto it, *or* you can *emotionalize* the joy of "walking fine" today, and then, you can look back at your childhood and go, "Wow! What a great childhood I had! That experience used to be my worst nightmare, in fact, it is my greatest strength. How awesome am I!"

Even knowing this, some people will *still* hang onto past bad experiences. They'll choose to use the association tool to stay stuck in their negative emotional pattern. *But, you've got to stop this temptation at the root—*

don't do it! Anytime you have a negative emotional thought pattern be very, very conscious about it, and ask, "Do I want to be miserable right now?"

Remember, our reality can be summarized as "now" versus "not now." Do you really want to be miserable *right now*?

Of course not!

Simply *dissociate* from your negative pattern.

Some people will get stuck here, they'll tell me, "Well, that's kind of manipulative. How can you do that? That just doesn't feel right to me."

My response to that—you are *already* using association and disassociation... but in a negative way. You currently have no problem manipulating the joy right out of your life because you're driven by a humility and humbleness program. You can't tell me that you won't do this because you have a problem with the idea. I just don't buy it. You are going to have to get deep into all the reasons *why* you do or don't do what you want in life. It's your choice, and it's who you *decide* to be—which leads me to another important tool...

Identity Statements

Your identity is your unconscious definition of yourself, which is something you protect very fiercely when challenged. It all starts with two simple words—"I am." Think about those words for a second and feel what they mean to you, "I am."

From an NLP (Neuro-Linguistic Programming) standpoint, this is the single, most powerful, self-programming tool that you have. When you say the words, "I am," whatever follows becomes a law. It becomes a fact, and it defines your reality. Some identity statements make perfect sense. You might say, "I am a Caucasian," "I am Hispanic," "I am Asian," "I am male," or "I am female."

Well, you're not going to wake up tomorrow and be a different race or a different gender, so that won't change your reality too much.

But, what if you say something like, "I am lazy," "I am a procrastinator," "I am not good," or "I am terrible?"

If I asked you to give me an identity statement around your health, you might say, "Oh, I am not in great shape." An identity statement for your finances might be, "Oh, gosh, I am always losing money," "I better be careful, I lose money easily," or "I better be careful or the planet will take money away from me."

Embedded in each of these commands is the "I am" statement defining *who you are.*

What if, when I asked you about your health, you said, "I have an amazing immune system!"

Now is that true or false? If you're alive today, I'll tell you what—you definitely have an amazing immune system even if you're sick. Your body is constantly assaulted by germs, viruses, and toxins every day, yet without even having to *think* about it, your immune system cleans, fights, grows, heals, and rejuvenates. Trust me; you definitely have an *amazing* immune system.

When was the last time you said, "I have an incredible, magical, amazing immune system I'm totally in love with?"

Unfortunately, when all you focus on is, "I'm overweight," or "I'm not in great shape," your brain will create that for you. You have an unconscious mind-body connection, and when you look at these command structures, "I am" takes on great power. As such, "I am an amazing immune system" can also become a powerful new identity. As your mind moves to this new focus, your weight and health will also start to shift.

Similarly, what if you said, "Money is always flowing to me! I just ask for it, and it shows up."

Now, some of you are going to say, "Well, wait a second, Bill. That doesn't happen to me."

I'm going to challenge you on this. When was the last time you made a statement such as that? When was the last time you held *the identity,* "I am abundant?" When was the last time you held the identity you can tap into the potential of the universe? Why does the universe give you money? Because you ask for it, because you believe in it, and because you're a great person who deserves money. Instead, many people who struggle with money and finances have created an identity that says, "I'm poor. I'm fighting my bills. I'm not rich." But then, they sit there and say, "Well, I'd like to be rich *someday.*"

This just won't cut it. You've got to program yourself to be rich, and it all begins with the identity statement process.

Now interestingly, if I ask you about parenting, you will probably be a little bit more charitable because you really do love your kids. You'll say things like, "I am a good parent," or even, "I am a great parent," and those positive identity statements *do* set you up to win. However, here's what also usually happens. Most people will say they are good parents, but they don't fully believe it. They beat themselves up for all the little things they are not doing well enough or not doing at all. They unconsciously catalog all the things they don't do 100% perfectly. If you are like most people, you have probably been unconsciously taught and told that *if* you change what you do and demonstrate certain attributes, *then* (and only then), can you say something nice about yourself.

That's backwards. You have to change how you *talk* about yourself first, and then it's easy to change who you are. You can now say to yourself, "You know what? I do have an incredible immune system. I have great health, and I release excess weight. I am a magical parent. Maybe, I occasionally do some silly things, but hey, that's the fun part of me."

Trust me, this mindset will not only benefit *you*, but it will make a huge positive impact on your kids, as well. When your children see you coming from a place of power, it will help them build their own self esteem, as well. If you explain the technology behind creating positive "I am" statements, they can also learn to program themselves to own some big adjectives.

This is a tool you can both use forever, and everything will begin to shift when you create an incredible, Level 10 identity statement.

I have *one* more tool for you in this section...

Values & Rules

I've chosen to put this piece last because it's fun, easy, and you'll understand its capabilities quickly. This is not a complex or complicated tool, but it does relate back to the questions you answered about your blueprint in Chapter 1.

- Who are you <u>right now</u>? (Be as specific as possible—this is your current mental snapshot and it's a vital part of *The Inevitable You®* system.)

- What is your world view?

- Complete these sentences. I am..., Strangers are..., The world is....

- What do you <u>really</u> want? Do you want a better relationship? A better job? A better career? Do you want to be a better parent? Do you want better health? What has to happen for you to get that?

- What do you <u>not</u> want in life? What has to happen for you to experience that?

- If I gave you all the money, all the time, and all the resources to create your life, what are your dreams? What are your visions? What do you really want for yourself?

I hope that you answered these questions back in Chapter 1 as the "old you" because this is the place where you'll be able to really see an incredible contrast between the "old you" and the "new you."

Values are the emotions and qualities of life you want or don't want, and your rules are what it takes for you to get there.

For example, you might say you value freedom, love, safety, or adventure. However, you might have conflicting rules about how to get there. You might want adventure, but only when you feel safe. Or, you might value love, but only if your loving gestures towards others are equally returned.

When you answered the questions from Chapter 1, one of the things you probably said that you want in life is more money. When you think about it now, do you really want money? Or, do you want the way you think money will make you *feel*? You want what money can *bring you*, whether that is security, freedom, pride, or self-esteem.

Think about this—if you could create the feeling you want to get from money, and you can do it forcefully and consistently, isn't that true power? Doesn't that give you *authentic* greatness? And here's how crazy, counterintuitive this stuff is. If you want joy, happiness, and ecstasy, the "old you" probably believed that you needed the evidence in the form of dollar bills in order to have those emotions and feelings. But, have you ever required any evidence to take on all the feelings you don't want? You have no pre-requisite for feeling anxiety, fear, or frustration.

Your "rules" to feel all of these emotions have been easy, right? What about your emotions around those experiences? Was your EIM high or low? Go back and look at what you wrote down. Chances are, you used to make it easy to experience all the things you don't want in life and very difficult to appreciate progress towards what you *want* in life.

When I did this exercise with Tony Robbins ten years ago, I sat down, and I said "I want to be happy." Then, I wrote down my rules for happiness. I said, "Well, I live in Colorado. I live here in part for the sunshine. So, I need a beautiful sunrise and big blue skies in the morning. That really makes me happy. When I go to work, I need traffic to be good. I don't like stop-and-go traffic. I get really frustrated in stop-and-go traffic. I don't want that. I want smooth and easy traffic flowing right to my business office. And, I also want to be able to successfully maintain my sales job while coaching clients full time. I need to close all the deals I make and to make all my clients happy."

Now I want you to think about this. If I'm driving to work and there are grey skies, am I happy? I don't even control the skies! And, if the sunrise doesn't look perfect, I am also upset. What the sunrise looks like is completely out of my control! And, do I control traffic either? Even if there was a beautiful sunrise and clear skies, but slow traffic, I was *still* frustrated! It didn't stop there. When I got to work, I was always on edge and in fear about whether or not my contracts would all be signed. I was constantly just waiting for a deal to get pulled out from underneath me.

With these expectations, what do you think the probabilities were that I was happy most of the time? Do you think it was easy for me to be happy? Conversely, how hard was it for me to get upset, stressed, and frustrated? The emotional intensity attached to my happiness was dissociated and small because I just waited for the planet to play a trick on me, and the emotional intensity attached to my frustration was bright, fully associated, and large. I constantly looked and waited for bad news. There just had to be clouds in the sky. There just had to be one traffic accident. There just had to be one cog in the machine of all the things that were in motion to pay me my commission check. One little cog in the system could have one little slip, and boom—I would be unhappy, frustrated, and full of anxiety.

And, here's what's really ironic. If you would have asked me during this time, "Bill, are you happy?" I would have responded, "Yes," because even in my confused "old you" state, I knew I was still much happier than a lot of people around me. But I wasn't yet the "new me," I wasn't at a Level 10, and I wasn't in joy and ecstasy. I was certainly doing the best I could with the tools I had available at the time, but I didn't even know what I was missing.

So, now here's the "new me" that I rewired ten years ago. My rules for joy, happiness, and ecstasy are now as follows: "When I wake up and there's a beautiful Colorado sunrise, a beautiful blue sky, or if I remember a sunrise anytime in the last week or simply look at the picture of a beautiful sunrise on my screensaver, then I'm happy. When I go to work, I won't stress or pressure myself even when the traffic is bad. Traffic's not in my control anyway. I'm just thrilled I'm in a car with gas! I love my car, and I always have great music playing. When, I'm at work, it doesn't matter if my client always loves a contract or not. It doesn't matter if the right attorney or CEO has signed my proposal or not because—I'm a Level 10 guy. I make deals happen. When I ask for deals, they come, and I've got a whole pipeline of deals sitting here. If any *one* of these things happen this morning, I'm going to experience full Level 10 happiness, joy, and ecstasy because that's where I'm going to place my focus, my thoughts, my feelings, my intention, and my beliefs."

Do you think this version of me had a whole lot easier time experiencing happiness than the old me?

In addition to making it much easier to be happy, I also made it very difficult for me to be upset. In order for me to get even the most minor amount of frustration in my life, a lot of things now have to happen. There has to be grey skies, I have to try and experience a memory of a sunset and that has to completely fail, my screensaver has to not work, and I have to look at the weather forecast and see that there is no sun coming soon. I have to really, really focus hard, work hard, and absolutely ensure that I cannot experience a great sunrise. Only if *all* that happens, may I place a small amount of frustration on the day. But, in order to be upset, I also need for the traffic to be terrible; it has to be the worst traffic jam I've ever been in, and it has to make me super, crazy late. And, when I try to make a deal, *everybody* has to hate me, and my future pipeline for new business has to be completely dead.

These rules make it *very* difficult for me to upset.

Again, I will get nay-sayers who tell me, "Oh Bill, it seems so disingenuous that you make it easy to be happy and so hard to be unhappy," and I'm like, "Yeah, that's the point!"

That's the point. Make it easy to be happy, and make it hard to be unhappy.

Realize that for most of your life you've probably been doing the opposite because that's what your family of origin taught you, and there was a benefit to it. Maybe it saved you some disappointment, maybe you weren't hurt when the world was mean to you, or maybe you never had to risk getting your hopes up.

Whatever benefits the "old you" received because of those strategies, your life as the "new you" can be much deeper, fulfilling, and richly textured than you ever imagined. Once you fully embrace this new way of being, you'll say, "Holy smokes! Why would I have ever been the 'old me.' I'm smarter than this! I'm better than this! I can do this! I am a Level 10 guy! I am a Level 10 woman! I can do this! I can make easy rules to create happiness and joy all the time, and I can make frustration, anxiety, and uncertainty really hard to even creep into my world. And, if anything bad happens, I'm going to look really deeply at it so I can see what is both half full *and* half empty. I understand how to define the meaning I will take out of every moment. I am conscious and aware. I know I'm not perfect, I know I'm going to fall a lot, and I know that as long as I am my authentic self, this will all ultimately lead to my ultimate greatness. *I am inevitable.*"

Do you now understand at a deeper level why "Don't spill the milk," became "Don't lose the deal?" Do see how much better your world will be if you set yourself up to win instead by declaring, "I'm a winner," and then tell yourself to simply, "Pour the milk carefully?"

This is the difference between successful overachievers and those who struggle in life. As I have told you before, they're not better, smarter, or more talented than you—they just use different recipes. They think differently, and they approach life differently.

You can experience a new reality in a single instant simply by thinking differently and by finding a new focus. You now have a roadmap to create an entirely new day tomorrow. You no longer have any excuses. Don't be asleep, don't be unconscious, and don't pretend you're unhappy because the planet, or your spouse, or the economy made you that way. If you are broken, you will only be stronger than before. Celebrate. *You are the "new you!"*

- Who are you right now?

- What is your world view?

- Complete these sentences. I am..., Strangers are..., The world is....

- What do you <u>really</u> want? Do you want a better relationship? A better job? A better career? Do you want to be a better parent? Do you want better health? What has to happen for you to get that?

- What do you <u>not</u> want in life? What has to happen for you to experience that?

- If I gave you all the money, all the time, and all the resources to create your life, what are your dreams? What are your visions? What do you really want for yourself?

Compare these answers to your responses in Chapter 1.

CHAPTER FOURTEEN:
Party of Three, Please

As your greatness expands, so does your fear.

Before I go any further, I need to lay some important groundwork. Remember when I told you that as a West Point, military man, I am passionately devoted to completing a mission? Well, this chapter is case in point.

As I've personally evolved and started to connect the dots in the "change and transformation" field, along the way I have realized some of the key distinctions I have made don't come as easily to everyone, and, to be honest, it used to bug me that people didn't seem to just "get" all of this information. I've had enough first-hand experiences to cement this knowledge in my psyche to the point where it's hard to even fathom another way of being. As the great Oliver Wendell Holmes explained, "A mind, once expanded, never goes back to its original dimensions."

And so, I've come to realize that I've been blessed with an eclectic background encompassing several aspects of life and that most people have not yet been privileged with this diverse perspective and natural pool of knowledge.

But, in order to complete my mission, I had to figure out a way to break the code. What was going on inside people to make change and transformation so hard? I had to figure out a way to make this sync for *everyone.*

Here's what I discovered.

I learned that as people evolve, they hear, learn, and understand things very differently. You see, the "old you" is truly an entirely different person than the "new you," and now we need to introduce another "you." The "greatest version of you" is a completely new being, as well. You may have experienced this view of you. Maybe you rose to an occasion for your child or someone you loved who really needed you. Maybe you really wanted something at one point in your life, and you got it. The "greatest version of you" is that part of you who shows up at Level 10 to create reality. Your world as the "old you" was limited, and you could only handle so much with this limited perspective.

Avoiding failure used to be one of your biggest drivers, right? You used to blame others, or yourself, for failures. Alternatively, you may have had a passive-aggressive attitude about it, right? Surely, by now you've accepted that failure really does lead to growth even though it doesn't always feel that way in the moment. As your reality has now shifted, I know that you're ready for more. The "new you" is open to learning at a much higher level.

It's kind of like one of those old Polaroid cameras. The ones where you took the picture, pulled it out, and then watched it develop into a great photo in your hand. Do you remember those? Think of it this way— whereas as the "old you" is the finite photo; the "new you" is the negative. While some concepts you'll hear in this section are identical at their core to some you heard previously as the "old you"; you're now able to understand them in an even more empowering way. Therefore, as I bring up a topic we've somewhat "covered" before, don't stop reading and say to yourself, "Oh, I've heard this before." You are in a new psychology. You are an entirely different person now. Instead ask, "How will the 'new me' absorb and translate this material?"

Understanding this natural evolution in thinking has cleared up a lot of confusion for my clients, and it has answered my query as to why so many of you *don't change* even when given all the right tools. By making these distinctions, you and I can both determine who's talking, who's asking, and who's answering questions. Which version of you is in the driver's seat? In the middle of a session, I'll often ask a client things like, "Who just said that," "Who just had that thought," and "Exactly who am I talking to?"

Once my clients get this, they understand their own psyche better, as well. When they fall back after experiencing a new challenge, they look sheepishly at me and say, "Oh, I guess that was the 'old me' popping off again."

And, I'll say "Right on!"

So, the next time you sit down at the table to think through one of your life's puzzles, just remember, you are a "party of three" and respond accordingly.

- When do you fall back into "old you" patterns and thinking?

- Describe the "new you" so that you'll know when this version of you is really in control.

- What do you feel as you think and process the "greatest version of you"?

PART 3:

The "Greatest Version of You"

CHAPTER FIFTEEN:
The Greatest You

Climb a tower to the highest platform
you can stand… and go one more.

How does the "new you" feel now?

We've come a long way together, my friend.

We have honored, respected, and definitively released, the "old you," we have wiped out your old programs and old patterns, we have given the "new you" a new reality and perspective, and we have shared an extensive array of amazing and empowering tools.

So, what's next?   What more could there be?

Put your seatbelts on. It's time to move into the "greatest version of you."

The Psychological Cycle of Life

Becoming the "greatest version of you"—how does that sound? Great! Maybe a bit scary, right? But, it's also exciting, adrenalizing, and dynamic! It all starts in your mind.

As you think about the blueprint process, I want you to put a circle in your mind and pick a point within it around the 9-o-clock point. This is where you're at right now. You've come full circle and are stepping into a completely new version of yourself. However, you're not "finished." In fact, you'll never stop growing and evolving—that's the purpose of life. You are now spiraling upwards and you are at the start of an entirely *new cycle* of transformation. During our time together, you've covered a lot of ground. You now understand that reality hasn't been happening to you. It's just that the "old you" designed by your family of origin was unconsciously running the show.

But, you've changed all that, and you are now operating under your own chosen mindset.

The next point on the circle is what I call ICM, or "I choose meaning." It's at 12-o-clock. From there, your psychology has been moving you clockwise forward toward the programs, strategies, recipes, and methods that you choose to use. (By the way, these programs can also work in reverse as filters that prevent you from seeing all of your available resources.) From there, you've decided which actions to take. However, you will inevitably run into fear at around 3-o-clock, and at this point you have three choices—you can work backwards and take new actions in a futile attempt to avoid fear, you can move past fear by taking *no* actions (which will leave you stagnant, un-evolved, and in the same, mundane cycle), or you can *embrace fear*, create more awareness, and elevate to your next level.

Bottom line—you are in a continual process that either revolves in a repetitive circle or advances as a spiral upwards with new growth.

Your Programs & Subprograms

Remember, your life is like a software program, and your goal is to make constant upgrades. It doesn't matter what version of software your mind is currently running, you need to update it regularly. You also need to continually update and refine your subprograms. Earlier, I explained how your subprograms can show up as "Towards and Away" patterns, but they also dynamically represent how you handle health, love, money, and all other aspects of your life. For example, you could be stuck in a very old money pattern, but your love pattern could be very effective and up to date. Or, your health subprogram might be very up to date, but because you're experiencing a divorce, your love subprogram might be corrupted. Making sense?

So when you look at your overall life, it's nothing more than a diverse tapestry depicting all of your patterns, strategies, and subprograms combined—the completed masterpiece yields *you*. All of your subprograms lead to who you are at any given moment. You could be *feeling great* one day, but then a job or health scare could present a new challenge that shifts everything.

That's why those pivotal moments are what define you. How you choose to act *after the act* is your opportunity to shift to a new level of the growth spiral. You get to decide to take a stand on where you want your life to be. You can say, "I'm going to be the greatest version of me possible," *or* you can say to yourself, "I'm going to think about it. I'm going to reflect on it. I'm going to wake up tomorrow morning and still be who I am today... because I'm not ready to change today. I think I should go for it, but I'm not sure yet."

Wherever your life is, it is based on the actions that you take on a daily basis. If your life presents a challenge or throws a big economic,

147

relationship, or health storm at you, you will simply react the best that you know how. That's what 90% of the planet is busy doing.

It's also why you *must* approach things differently.

Going from the "old you" to the "new you" was like turning on a light switch. You just needed the awareness to know that you needed to flip on the switch and some tools to help bring you into the light. You don't need to spend months or years to become the "new you." It literally happened in a snap. And, from this illuminated, powerful position, you can launch (equally fast) into the "greatest version of you."

How cool is that?

The reason why I selected the title the "greatest version of you" to explain this aspect of yourself is because it holds a very simple truth that everybody understands—we all know that we have the power to give things our "best." We inherently understand this when we operate as our greatest self. In fact, at this point, anytime you're not operating as the "greatest version of you," you're probably consciously resting or relaxing into the realities of the "new you."

Thus, whether coming from a place of pain, improvement, or achievement, we all know where we stand in relation to how close we are to our greatness. It's an amazing standard to take a look at your life and to consistently judge it against what's possible as the "greatest version of you."

Try it on for a moment. How does it feel?

The Trapeze

I think that the metaphor of a trapeze best represents this idea, and here's why. When you move from the "old you" to the "new you," and now to the "greatest version of you," your fear level continues to go up in direct proportion with your level of advancement. As a result, when you elevate to the "greatest version of you," your fear is going to shoot out of sight. It's going to be crazy and intense. You will feel anxious and unconfident, and you'll think to yourself, "Can I do this? I'm now climbing a new part of the mountain—it's hard! I'm in a place I've never been! I've never even pictured myself being here!"

Have you ever seen the TV show, *Circus of the Stars*? Although they had a lot of acts, the most thrilling was always the trapeze act because it's one of the scariest and most difficult. The celebrities on the show would deliver their performance 40 feet off the ground, and they would dramatize the whole experience on TV by showing several dynamic camera angles. It all made for breathtaking, awe-inspiring footage. The handsome star or the beautiful starlet would leap out towards the trapeze, and everybody in the audience would be in a trance and on the edge of their seats. Would the hero or heroine successfully catapult into a graceful trick, or would he or she fall into disheveled failure? It was all very exciting to see.

Well—right now, *you are the star*. And to discover the "greatest version of you", here's what you must do. You must climb your tower to the tallest platform you can handle *and then you must go up one more.* You must stand in this tiny tower platform to make your giant leap. You are going to be clutching your stomach and feeling weak in the knees, but you must stay strong because there's more.

Even though it's scary, you must also remove your personal safety net. The "greatest version of you" cannot be afraid to fall. What's more? You must also remove the big burly catcher who's swinging over on the opposite trapeze—he can't be there either. You are creating the "greatest version of you," not the greatest version of his catch. If he slips, if his hands are sweaty, or if he's thinking about his grocery list instead of catching you, you will not be able to become the "greatest version of you." Your ultimate success cannot be left to the mercy of someone else. And last, you must remove the trapeze over there, too. The "greatest version of you" is limited on this side of the leap by your life experiences here. You must leap and believe that you will create a new trapeze when you get to the other side! Got it? Good.

Now, you are ready.

It's time to take a leap of faith. You must launch forward, let go, and never look back. You must go the full distance! You must do so with total conviction, utter confidence, and sheer determination. The "greatest version of you," by natural law, cannot see the trapeze that will catch you. You must jump blind, but your greatness will create exactly what you need exactly where it needs to be the moment you arrive.

The "greatest version of you" always knows how to succeed. You will naturally find your balance and catapult into a new place—as long as you trust in yourself.

As you leap into the "greatest version of you," you will become a new person—again! You will start to think new thoughts, have new feelings, and take new actions. Although this may be one of the most terrifying leaps you have ever made in life, you must have faith that all the resources you need will show up exactly when you need them.

And, even if they don't show up, you must still believe that you are on the right path. You must understand that you needed the growth more than you needed the exhilaration of success. You *needed* the lesson more than the victory. Even if you fall big, it will be with purpose, and it will bring you closer to your ultimate goals. Finally, also know that nothing will ever happen that you cannot handle.

Launched into this space of faith and growth, the "greatest version of you" will always find its natural resting place. You will always find your natural home, and you will come to know a sense of peaceful fulfillment that comes with that. Beyond the abyss of your greatest challenge, you are in a powerful, solution-driven universe. Acknowledge your own faith and certainty and then use these pivotal tools to reinforce the truth that you already know deep inside—the "greatest version of you" is capable of soaring where nobody else waits, where nobody else dares to go, and were nobody else even believes is possible.

When you get there, congratulations! You will have finally stepped into the "greatest version of you." But beware—there is no turning back from here!

- Who is the "greatest version of you"?

- Does stepping into the "greatest version of you" elicit a sense of fear or a sense of excitement in you?

- What does it mean in your life to take a leap of faith into what's possible as the "greatest version of you"?

CHAPTER SIXTEEN:
Preparing for Your Greatness

To whom much is given, much is expected.

As you leave parts of both the "old you" and the "new you" behind and leap towards the "greatest version of you," what you are really doing is letting go of more patterns. Whereas the "old you" was based on unconscious patterns that stem from your family of origin, the "new you" was based on conscious choices to take control of your life and the direction in which it's moving.

So, at this point, I want you to really look at which part of you just defined the "greatest version of you" in the questions at the end of the last chapter. Whatever vision you wrote down, I want to challenge you to raise the bar even more. Did you truly write about a Level 10 version of you? Or, was it really a seven or eight because expecting you to live up to a ten felt too scary, greedy, or hard? You may not completely "get it" right now, but I want you to completely ELIMINATE those limitations RIGHT NOW, *right at the beginning of this process.*

The "old you" originally never even had a vision of the "greatest version of you," and the "new you" likely doesn't know what you are fully capable of accomplishing. There may have been some brief moments when the "new you" experienced your full greatness. You may have succeeded against the odds in the past, but it hasn't been happening consciously or consistently. Now, it's time to make your greatest vision a reality.

You've done a lot of work already, but there is definitely more. I do not want you to walk away from this book until you've both realized and owned your full, true potential. Remember—mission first, *mission always*.

I am committed to walk this final, exhilarating, stretch of a mile with you. I just need you to go there with me. So, right now, I need you to commit to taking on an even deeper level of consciousness as you continue reading in order to fully absorb all that is coming. Are you ready?

In order to get to *your place of true, authentic greatness*, there are now three key patterns (aka, programs) you will need to identify and learn to manage. Understanding these three programs is the vital foundation that will help you stay anchored in your vision of greatness. These three programs are, "Fear Management," "Failure Management," and "Sabotage Elimination."

1. Fear Management

Fear management is very simple. You may believe that when you eliminate an obstacle, you will automatically receive a corresponding breakthrough that will dilute your fear and anxiety. This idea definitely makes sense. However, there is just one counterintuitive (but vital) issue with the notion.

Having fear present is an essential ingredient necessary for greatness. As soon as you have no fear, you're no longer progressing. Although you might take a moment to catch your breathe between great climbs, ultimately, as soon as you've conquered one peak, you are going to want to climb to another part of the mountain! That's the way life works. There's always more to discover, more boundaries to push, and more new experiences to explore. To be living in constant greatness is to experience a level of constant excitement that surpasses anything you've ever known!

Here is the key (and, by the way, one of the most important concepts you will read in this book). If you are a seminar or self-help junkie, this may be one of the biggest reasons why you've left your life unfinished (in spite of having access to so much great information). In order to move to the next phase of your ultimate greatness, *you must successfully integrate all your new knowledge*.

Often, this is easier said than done. Here's why. When you try to integrate new knowledge into your existing sphere of life, your fear and anxiety will inevitably rise. However, instead of realizing that this feeling is normal and expected, you'll probably think to yourself, "Gee, I must not have this right. I must not get it. This isn't working the way I expected."

Then, you'll retreat back to your old comfortable self. You'll walk away from what is possible and retreat to familiar territory and old patterns. If you thought that it was hard to step into and own the "new you," the tendency to give up is even more common as you contemplate living up to your *greatest* potential. That's a huge standard to take on. But, you can do it. *It all relies on your focus.* Your ability to manage your fear right now is uber-critical.

Beyond fear, you may also be experiencing something better described as "anxiety." This corresponding anxiety is related to your fear, but it stems from a different program. Whereas your fear comes from an "old you" protection pattern, your anxiety is actually a sense of excitement about what's coming. It's rooted in your greatness, and this is new territory for you. Remember—all heroes, all overachievers, and all successful people on this planet have fear and anxiety. But, they also know how to manage their failure. They also have great fear and anxiety *management* techniques. Remember the 800-foot cliff climber. While she had "fear" what she really had was adrenaline, and she called that "life." This is where the "greatest version of you" will live.

Got it?

Moving on...

2. Failure Management

Failure at this level looks something like this—as you step up higher on the trapeze platform of life, you risk higher and higher heights of failure. The stakes go up, the view gets more intimidating, and the technical difficulty gets intense. You may feel like you are going to fall *more*, and you may intuitively realize that if (and when) you do fall, it will be more severe.

But remember, in order to get the gold medal in life, you have to seek out the double-black-diamond runs. You have to take yourself down the scariest slopes on the mountain, and you have to trust yourself to make it down even when the conditions are icy, cold, or blizzard-ridden. It may scare the living daylights out of you, but you absolutely _can_ conquer whatever is holding you back as long as you maintain a top-of-the-line, amazing failure management strategy. Trust me on this.

Next?

3. Sabotage Elimination

Lastly, the "greatest version of you" must ask *every day*: "Is the action I am taking or not taking today going to enhance my greatness, or am I sabotaging myself?"

Sabotage is a very unique aspect of your psyche. Unlike other self-help authors or psychologists, I like to highlight this pattern because I hold *you* responsible for *your* greatness, and I will not let you off the hook. If you embrace a psychology of sabotage (meaning taking actions that do not enhance you or add value to your life), you might as well stop reading. These actions will not help you grow to a champion level; they will penalize you and hold you back.

However, to be clear, I want to make sure you understand the difference between sabotage and failure. What if you create an action plan for investing, but you then procrastinate in doing the needed research to follow-through? Sabotage or failure? Yep—sabotage.

What if you *did* the research, invested regularly, but somehow kept losing money? Correct. Failure, but necessary to succeed.

What if you start working towards your plan, stop, then start again, and then stop again—what is that? If you are braking because you think that you might be going too fast, is that failure or sabotage? What if you are *not stopping* even though you are overwhelmed, and as a result, you're not really absorbing the lessons in your path?

This is where sabotage gets a bit more interesting. These two paths have similar consequences, yet a very different psychology drives them.

If you find yourself putting on the brakes from time to time, your patterns may not be setting you up to win. However, rather then stopping completely and mindlessly beating yourself up for it, simply decide to slow down. As important as it is to work past your fears, it's equally important to capture the lessons and to be aware of what's really going on when your progress halts.

Similarly, charging full steam ahead and ignoring the lessons along the way doesn't work either. You must also be fully conscious about what's happening along each step of your trajectory in order to integrate new lessons and truly advance towards your dreams.

I know this is a little confusing, but I want to make sure this subtle distinction sinks in for you. So, let me give you one more example.

As a parent (and if you don't have kids, think back to when you were a kid), imagine teaching your kids about their own greatness just before they go off to college. You tell them to reach for the stars simply because *you* believe in them, which is awesome. However, will that really serve them when they're faced with the first challenges they must conquer all on their own? It will help a little, for sure. But ultimately, they will have to develop their *own* internal patterns and belief systems in order to progress. You're going to have to assume that what they will use as a model is *your belief systems*—for better or worse. Therefore, if you want to know what will happen when your kids are off on their own, simply ask *yourself*, "Did I reach for the stars when I was their age?"

And even more importantly, "Am I reaching for the stars, *right now, today*?"

However you answer this question and however you see that pattern realistically playing out in your children will tell you everything you need to know about your current pattern of greatness. You can *tell* your kids to reach for the stars, but if you are leading by example with sabotage, that's what your kids will do, as well. If you tell them that anything's possible, but then showcase a careful, safe, and cautious life, they will only be able to enjoy the same level of conditional greatness that you've demonstrated.

Let me tell you loud and clear—if your dream is dead right now, your kids' dreams are in big trouble.

Let's review. Failures are inevitable and needed, fear and anxiety can translate to excitement, mindful progress is mandatory, and all sabotage patterns *must be eliminated forever.* Got it?

I know it's a lot, but all of this simply takes practice. The more you embody these principles, the clearer it will all become.

In the meantime, here's a trick to help you manage all your patterns, good and bad.

Patterns to Interrupt Patterns

Here's how it works. Old patterns come from old programs, old strategies, and old recipes, right? Old patterns are the old thoughts that hold you back, and they contain the old interpretation that you "can't," "won't," or "don't," right? This is how old patterns show up in your thoughts. Remember when we talked about that "old song on the radio"? We discussed how a song could come on and instantly trigger a reaction unconsciously to completely shift your emotions—even if you were completely unaware of what was happening. Well, this can happen at a deeper level as the "greatest version of you" also. You could be walking through your office, talking to a friend, talking to a prospect, living a great life, when a voice comes from down the cubicle row that sounds just like your abusive father. You may not hear it consciously, but guess what does? So *all of a sudden* your brain might tell you, "I don't feel very good right now. There's danger around me; there's a problem."

If this happens to you, you should definitely listen, pause, and evaluate your intuition. Inner-instinct is never something to gloss over. However, be sure to look deeply behind what's driving the sudden fear. Nine times out of ten, it will be rooted in an old trigger that your unconscious mind picked up on. Your unconscious self heard "that old song on the radio" even though you walked by and didn't even notice, and as a result, you're neural peptides and adrenaline levels have all started to rise. Your unconscious mind will be saying, "This is a bad moment for me," but your conscious mind will say, "Wait a second, I am focused on my greatness right now. What's the problem?"

So, here's the good news—breaking an old pattern is easy at this stage. In order to interrupt an old pattern, you simply have to recognize that it's happening. Sometimes you'll know exactly where it's coming from, and other times, you won't even care. You just need to recognize what's going on and then return to your greatness. End of story.

Just one more point of caution—there are a few ways your old pattern could show up. Besides some old song or other external trigger, your pattern could be an old fear, an old truth, or an old identity statement that sneaks into your mind. Sometimes, it might even be a *new fear,* but, once you realize what's happening, you can literally simply soar over the abyss.

Awareness is the key. Your "greatest version of you" psychology can handle the rest.

- What are the great thoughts that the "greatest version of you" must have to fulfill your vision for what's possible?

- What are the great emotions attached to those thoughts?

- As a consequence of those great thoughts and emotions, what great actions will the "greatest version of you" take?

- What are you anxious about at this point?

- How can you turn those feelings into a sense of excitement?

CHAPTER SEVENTEEN:
Your Greatest Vision

Are you breathing your Greatness? Are you feeling it shake all the way to the core of your spine?

So, what is your vision of the "greatest version of you"? What tools are you using to create it? As you sit down at your "table for three," who's driving your own internal brainstorming session—is it the "old you," the "new you," or the "greatest version of you"?

Pretty soon, you are going to "choose meaning," and you are going to "choose action" for how you proceed moving forward from here, and you need to be absolutely certain that the "greatest version of you" is driving the bus when you get there. I know you've been thinking about your greatest possible self, and if you've been answering the questions at the end of each chapter (which I really hope you are), you should have already jotted down some thoughts about your "greatest you" vision. By now, I believe that you have the basis to truly uncover the destiny that is yours, to boldly declare the vision of the "greatest version of you," and to *mean* it!

However, although you have all tools needed to take your limitations and disempowering beliefs and to minimize them, your disempowering beliefs are not going to eventually just go away. Sorry! New and more subtle doubts will continue to pop up no matter how high you climb.

But, that is normal. Even though it sounds defeating, it's actually very positive, and it means you're on the right track.

One of my favorite authors, Cherie Carter Scott, explains it like this. She talks about the ten rules for being a human, and her fourth rule is my favorite. It says, "The purpose of being a human is to grow and to learn. Life will present you lessons, and as you learn these lessons, you will grow. If you do not learn the lessons, life will present them to you again, and again, and again. And, if you do not learn the lessons when they are presented, life will present them again, but make them harder, and harder, and harder. You will know that you've learned a lesson when your actions or behaviors change."

Being the "greatest version of you" is not about having a perfect standard or a perfect destination; it's about having a perfect 'towards" commitment and a perfect trajectory. The "greatest version of you" will never actually find a state of perfection because you are constantly going to be asking for more and more. You are going to want to live more, to experience more, to climb higher, and reach farther. A great number of things are going to start to happen as you develop your ideal life, commit to its path, and so, you must consistently remind yourself, "I want to experience life as the *greatest* version of me."

Take a moment now and think back again to the questions I asked you at the end of Chapter 1. What was the blueprint that you created for yourself at that stage? As the "greatest version of you," your entire description should have changed by now. You will naturally be using more interesting, bolder, and more powerful adjectives to describe your life. You will have broader, deeper, and more original ideas.

You are now on a pedestal, high on the trapeze of greatness. The rules, values, and habits that once held you back are now gone. The goals and outcomes that you set for yourself are full of emotional richness and texture.

It doesn't matter if the "old you" was a victim, a survivor, or a champion. It doesn't matter if the "new you" is still experiencing some present-day hardships. At this point, in spite of whatever you've experienced or are currently handling, you now have the capacity to take all the tools that you've learned in this program and to redesign your blueprint again. The "greatest version of you" is going to step up and embody your greatest vision. You are going to clearly see the greatest possible version of yourself. You will be focused on empowering, uplifting vibrant thoughts, and you will attach incredible emotions to all of your experiences.

Again, if you're really taking on this new role, it should scare the living bejeebers out of you. But, that's righteous, too. This is how you know you are truly stretching yourself to a new, powerful level. The "greatest version of you" will not turn back. You will not go back to that old life. You can no longer pretend to be a victim in any way. You can no longer blindly focus on "not spilling the milk." You have a new thought process now.

The "greatest version of you" is going to show up, it's going to scare the heck out of you, and it is going to be epic. A legend will be born. Maybe your legend will take the form of an incredible CEO, or perhaps your legend will be an incredible, rock–star, soccer mom. Your legend may be one of a beautiful Yogina, an incredible personal trainer, or a magical small business owner.

The choice is yours. Anything and everything is possible, and it's all at your fingertips.

Remember earlier when I asked you to rate how powerful, magical, and extraordinary you are on as scale of one to ten? I would be very surprised if you were at a 10 at that time. However, I *know* that you are at a 10 now. Now you know who you really are. Now you know the "greatest version of you." Do you see what I see? You are magnificent and beautiful. You now have the capacity to achieve whatever you set your mind towards. You are full of failure, full of fear, full of mistakes, full of growth, *and full of greatness.*

Now you have the ability to choose great strategies to *always* set yourself up to win. How powerful, magical, and extraordinary are you? You are human, remember? That means you have *unlimited potential.* You're one of us.

At this point, promise me you will completely annihilate any strategies that have continued to limit or plague you. I need for the "greatest version of you" and only the "greatest version of you" to pull this together by focusing only on the truth. So, here we go...

Is the "greatest version of you" in charge right now?

- Are you creating, are you co-creating with life at this stage?

- Are you focused on the beliefs that hold you back, or are you focused on the beliefs that motivate you?

Your "greatest you" blueprint:

- Who are you right now? (Be as specific as possible.)

- What is your world view? (Only answer as the "greatest version of you.")

- Complete these sentences. I am..., Strangers are..., The world is....

- What do you <u>really</u> want? Do you want a better relationship? A better job? A better career? Do you want to be a better parent? Do you want better health? What has to happen for you to get that?

- What do you <u>not</u> want in life? What has to happen for you to experience that?

- If I gave you all the money, all the time, and all the resources to create your life, what are your dreams? What are your visions? What do you really want for yourself?

CHAPTER EIGHTEEN:
Catastrophic Failure Management

Greatness never needs reassurance.
You may have doubts from time to time, but the
"greatest version of you" never loses its truth North.

At this point, you may be thinking, "Well, wait a second. I think I screwed this entire process up because I'm scared. I don't know if I really believe that I am as great as you think I am."

This is your hidden parenthesis (except me) showing up again. *All humans are inevitable—<u>including you</u>*. Remember?

When people consider personal development, self-help, growth, or transformation, one of the problems that they have in applying their new knowledge always comes back to one very simple hang-up. The reason why they buy books and go to seminars in the first place is because they believe that there is an obstacle or a challenge holding them back. They keep hoping that "someone else" will fix their problem, and in the climax of each experience, they probably at least feel better... for a short period of time.

Most authors and teachers out there are very good. They make you feel good, they provide interesting new information, and they bring up valuable points that stimulate deep reflection. However, as good as they are, here's what they don't teach you. They don't tell you how to resolve a very interesting phenomenon. So here it is—when you go back to your daily life with this unbelievably pure and powerful intention to implement everything you've learned in this book, you are going to face an equally powerful feeling of anxiety and fear.

I know I've been talking about this a lot in the past few chapters, but understanding its existence is *so* crucial to your future success. *This is the one thing that can stop you at this point.*

Your anxiety and fear as the "greatest version of you" is going to be off the charts. If you are feeling uncertain or awkward right now, that's normal. It would be strange if you didn't have that sensation at this stage.

In your greatest place of power, you must take this in and be *ready* to combat these feelings accordingly. Always have your "greatest version of you" patterns, thoughts, questions, and values ready and close at hand. In addition, you must *deeply feel* the enormity of this critical distinction. The "greatest version of you" is *bound* to fail. Expect it. Your fear is going to be intense, and you are going to be scared. But *at that very moment of your most intense fear,* you must be ready to tap into your greatest, authentic power. You must own your fear, integrate it, and ride it out until it ultimately becomes a further part of your DNA and future greatness.

Plus, just as you must be ready to access your power when things are in chaos, you also cannot get lazy when things are at a peak. You must maintain your standard for greatness at all times. The good and bad.

Does that make sense?

I want you to really think about this because it's counterintuitive, and it won't be easy when you're faced with reality.

You've been climbing the mountain of life, and you picked up this book at some point because you felt stuck. You may have been stuck for a month, a year, or a decade—it doesn't matter. You've had some sort of obstacle holding you back. But now, you've obliterated it, destroyed, and annihilated it. Congrats. You're excited, and you're ready to begin climbing your mountain again, which is great. You're starting to explore new territory, and you're now climbing in a place you've never seen before. You're going to be thinking *new* thoughts, creating *new* actions, and having *new* emotions. You're in a totally foreign, harder, and more elevated place.

Deeply feel this truth. Breathe deeply, and feel this truth in your core.

Now, here's the good news. Once you expect and anticipate fear, you will be able to mitigate it more easily. You'll be able to manage the emotions that will make you doubt your path, and you'll be well-equipped to simply brush off any disempowering thoughts that slip into your mind. Every day your fear will go down a little bit more because the more you develop and practice managing your emotional power, the more natural this process will become. Eventually, you will be fluent in positive, powerful, and "towards" patterns as you continue to hone your "greatest version of you" skills, thoughts, emotions, and feelings.

But, until you advance to that level, just know that you'll be scared at first. You just cannot give up and walk away when you get there. Deal?

It's like you are about to go live in a new banquet hall where all the kings and queens of society live. You have a new residence in this fine establishment, but it may take you a little while to get completely used to your new reality, okay?

That said, becoming *The Inevitable You*® is not about eliminating fears; it's not about becoming fearless. It's not about not feeling scared anymore or feeling safe. Becoming *The Inevitable You*® is about failure management. It's about knowing how to tackle fears as the "greatest version of you."

Have I drilled this point into your head?

Good. This may be the single biggest reason why you have been attending seminar after seminar and reading book after book, yet *still* been stuck. I really hope you are hearing me on this and taking it all in.

Which leads to me to another critical must...

Pursue Failure

Remember in the "Towards and Away" section when I emphasized the amazing Eleanor Roosevelt's great lesson? I credit her with one of my key foundation principles—that failure is *necessary* for success. I know we've covered that point (a lot). But, as the "greatest version you," I really need this to sink in even a little more.

Knowing how to resolve your failures is great, but at your highest level, you must actually learn to *pursue* failure management. Let me give you an example.

When I met Picabo Street back in 1996, she was working on a campaign to get children to wear ski helmets. If you're from Colorado, like me, or if you've been a skier for at least the past several years, you can probably remember a time when wearing helmets was dorky and stupid, right? Only geeks wore helmets. Okay. So now, fast forward to today—wearing helmets is now cool, decorative, and indicative of fast, risk-taking, advanced skiers and boarders.

Well, that psychology all began with Picabo Street back in 1996. She started a campaign back then that said, "Falling is the entry ticket to becoming an Olympic Gold Medalist."

When I met Picabo and asked her about her falls, she told me about some bone-crushing, ligament-tearing, 100-mile-an-hour train wrecks. They were vicious falls, atrocious, triple-black-diamond catastrophes.

And, when Picabo won the Gold Medal back in 1998, it was definitely because she was the only contender who could ski under the terrible conditions that day. The weather was bad and the slope was razor-slick ice. Half of her contenders played it safe by slowing down, and the other half fell down the mountain. But, when Picabo took her place in the starting gates, she did so with total confidence. This was her terrain. At one point, she skied in an almost inverted position, with one ski high and one low. She looked out of control and completely askew as she took a jump that propelled her about 50 feet in the air going 100 miles per hour down the mountain. When she came over the ridgeline, one of the announcers actually said, "Oh my God, Bob. I think she's going to die."

But, Picabo stuck the landing! She knew how to balance mid-air, she knew how to tackle a fall at its most trying peak, and she knew how to turn a virtual crash into a magical finish only because *she'd already taken herself there so many times before in practice.* This wasn't her first time navigating past the potential for intense failure—she had already fallen (hard) on her own time. *That* is why she was able to perform *and to win* an Olympic Gold Medal on that blistery, icy, difficult day.

And that is the *psychology of success in action, my friend.*

This is case in point of what I've been trying to tell you.

How you wire yourself to win is to not even worry about failure. Real champions *want* falls. They want to experience failure so that they can elevate their game even more and learn from it. They ski, tips down, over their edge, every day.

So, what's your approach? Are you taking on the mountain head-on? Or, are you still peaking over the edge and wallowing in everything that could go wrong?

Maybe you are a small business owner, an executive in a company, or someone at the beginning of his career; or perhaps, you are on a quest to find a man or woman with whom to fall in love. Are you willing to risk everything at this point to reach your goals? Are you willing to risk a broken heart, to ski down that triple-black-diamond slope of love, to put yourself out there? Are you willing to step up and to ask for the promotion you know you deserve, to start a new business venture, or to dive into a new project full force?

All those training days on the mountain when Picabo fell over and over again, do you think she always felt good about it? There were days that she didn't want to practice; there were days when her heart was pounding into her throat with fear. But, she did it anyway. She lived over her edge, and in doing so, she continued to advance into that *zone of greatness* that only champions understand. You must do the same. *Real champions know that failure and failure management is a critical part of their success.*

However, beyond failure, you need to know that you have another deeper counter-strategy at play. It's our old friend—sabotage.

There is a huge difference between someone who is pushing himself *to* the edge and falling and someone who is pushing himself *off* the edge in order to avoid failure. To sabotage yourself is to fail on purpose so that you don't have to experience what it would have felt like to fail. If you never really try; you can never really fail, right? Let me tell you something—*this sorry strategy never adds value, and it never makes you feel complete.*

How many of you have started a business model or a love relationship and when it begins to feel out of control, you fall for safety?

And, this leads me to one final principle...

Integrity

Do you believe that most families in today's society teach and encourage us to have integrity? If you are thinking that this is a trick question— you're right. It is.

Here's the sad truth.

I'll use a great story from my dear friend, Gary King. Imagine little Mary at age four going into the kitchen to help her mom make cookies as her powerful, extraordinary, magical self. Mary sees that her mom has finished making the cookies, but that she is no longer in the kitchen when Mary gets there. So, Mary goes ahead and helps herself to a steaming chocolate-chip cookie fresh out of the oven. She takes one cookie off the plate and eats it with total joy. Then, her mom comes into the kitchen and says, "Oh my gosh! Who ate a cookie?" Little Mary excitedly tells the truth, "I had the cookie, Mommy," she says.

In our typical society, do you think little Mary is punished or rewarded for telling her mom the truth?

Unfortunately, in most families, she is punished, right?

So now, fast-forward to next Saturday. Mom is making cookies again, and this time, they are little Mary's favorite—oatmeal raisin. So, when her mom isn't in the kitchen, Mary quickly gobbles one up, and again, her mom comes back into the kitchen and immediately asks, "Oh my gosh! Who ate a cookie?" This time little Mary is a little wiser. She responds, "Well, um, you better check little Billy's breath. I think I smelled cookie on his breath."

So now, Mom doesn't know for sure who had the cookie. And, does little Mary get punished or rewarded for lying? Mary is rewarded. She escapes the punishment she endured after the last cookie-eating incident and walks away scot-free.

Then little Mary grows up. She is now the Vice President of a large shoe company. One day, her boss comes in and says, "I've got this incredible great idea! We are going to do XYZ with our products in the next quarter, and it's going to be huge!" Now, Mary is the VP in charge, and she's pretty smart. She can see that this idea has some inherent problems, and so, she truthfully explains this to her boss. She says, "You know boss, I've gotta level with you. That's not going to work. That's a great concept, but you know, the systems aren't ready, the marketing isn't ready. Your brilliant idea just isn't going to work."

With all of her heart and a lot of intense sincerity, Mary basically tells her boss, "You're wrong."

And, does her boss reward or punish her for telling the truth? Yep! In most businesses, Mary is punished for speaking her truth. She is cast as a naysayer, a pessimist, and "not a team player."

As much as most companies would *like to think* that they encourage truth and honestly, they actually often reinforce dishonesty. Most employees have learned to tell their bosses "what they want to hear" rather than "what they need to hear."

For example, let's look at another parallel universe with the same scenario. Let's say Mary's boss comes in and tells Mary about his XYZ idea, and Mary goes "Oh yeah, that's awesome! Yeah, I think that idea will really work."

She then goes out of her office and tells her friends, "Oh, my gosh! You're not going to believe what our boss is trying to do. It is really dumb, but I have to support it." Then, even though she doesn't really believe in it, Mary will halfheartedly go about the process and move forward on her boss's dumb idea anyway.

And, as a result, Mary will now be rewarded for lying to her boss and telling him that his idea was good.

Here's one more example.

When a girlfriend asks a boyfriend, "Tell me the truth," do women actually reward men for telling them the truth? (Girls, be honest in answering this. I'm married to one, so I know what happens.) The truth is a lot of times they don't. But, men don't always reward women for telling them the truth either.

In our culture we say things like, "Well, I couldn't tell my mother-in-law the dish she made for dinner was awful. She asked me how it was, but I couldn't hurt her feelings. I'm not going to tell her it was awful."

The "greatest version of you" knows how to handle any situation with grace and authentic integrity. This part of yourself will always show up with sincerity as the little organic, powerful, little four-year-old that you once were—as long as you ask it to.

If your mother-in-law asks you, "So, what did you think of the dish?" You can say, as the "greatest version of you" and with complete integrity, "You know, it was the most incredible dinner, I loved the experience, and the effort you put into it all was extraordinary. I had a wonderful time."

Isn't that what she was really asking anyway? "Did you enjoy my house? Did you enjoy my hospitality?" If she really wants to know about the dish, and says, "Yeah, but what did you think of the dish?" Then, you can say, "Well you know, it didn't really float my boat. It wasn't the best for me, but again, what I really appreciate is the fact that you went to the trouble to get a new recipe. That's my take away from the dinner."

To speak truthfully and honestly is so liberating. And, by the way, being this authentic with others will give you the ability to be completely authentic and honest with yourself, as well.

Having this deep level of integrity is what will give you the power to ask yourself, "What is my life really about? Am I really focused on the greatest version of me? Am I really embodying great thoughts, great emotions, and great actions right now? Am I recognizing my struggles as old patterns? Am I effectively managing my fear and anxiety? Am I focused on the adrenaline of life?"

Your greatness will show up every day... as long as you do.

- How have you sabotaged yourself in the past? Did those techniques work?

- What is the truth of who you are as the "greatest version of you"?

- What does that life look and feel like to you?

CHAPTER NINETEEN:
Choose Meaning

Your history won't change, but its *meaning* *can.*

You are now going to take *everything* that we've done so far in this entire book and create a new meaning for your life. As the "old you," you used to believe that your history was fixed. You used to think that whatever happened to you in the past is the truth of who, what, and why you are who you are.

You used to not have the ability to say, "Wait a second. I'm going to create a different meaning. I'd like to change what this situation means to me."

You used to assume that whatever meaning you gave an experience as a child or adolescent is *still* what it must mean today. And, so the "old you" created patterns to protect you from ever having to experience that type of pain again. HOW you arrived at being you today was once predicated on your THEN. Back in the day, you would go to a professional to tell them about your painful history and why it has turned you into who you are today, and a kind-hearted, well-intentioned person would love you unconditionally and simultaneously reinforce the root of your real problem.

Not any more. *This used to be your reality.*

Your world has been shaken up. You know that the reality of who you once thought you were is not who you are really are.

This chapter is about pulling it *all* together.

Half-Full & Half-Empty

You now know that *all* experiences are neither completely good nor completely bad. They are always simultaneously half-full and half-empty. And so, I have a small assignment for you.

Look back at chapter one, and look at your responses. Were the majority of your answers half-full or half-empty? Go back and write down the "other half" of each of these responses. How were each of your responses both half-full and half-empty? Look for the full picture.

Design New Meaning

Looking back at your past, you now also understand that _you_ get to decide which meaning you want to select. You can decide to make the half-empty version small, distant, and silent. You can choose to make the half-full meaning vibrant, alive, bright, and intimately close. This is what I want you to do next...

As the "greatest version of you," write a giant paragraph describing your new story based on the meanings you have chosen.

The Blueprint

You can now take anything, absolutely *anything* that's plagued you in life, and transform it into *incredible* power. You get to *choose meaning* from now and forever into the future, and this... is an extraordinary gift.

This is not a dream, or motivational, self-improvement mumbo-jumbo.

This is who you now are. You can play your half-full, inspiring movie *as many times as you want*! You can play it as often as you used to play your sad, half-empty story—or even more. It's real. It's your truth.

This is the adrenaline of life! It's what you have been working so hard to achieve.

There is just one more step.

CHAPTER TWENTY:
Choose Action

*You must JUMP and believe that your wings
will work in order to have the life you seek.*

What are you actually going to *do* today, tomorrow, and well into the future to embody all that you now know? What actions will you take? How will your actions change? Are you going to get a new job? Are you going to change your eating or exercise habits? Are you going to start dating, or will you make a change in your current relationship?

What will you do now?

As I have said before, most people's action is, unfortunately, to take no action at all.

Not you. The "greatest version of you" is on fire! You're ready to go. You are going to close this book, race out of your office or off your couch to act, to do, and to be... the "greatest version of you"!

In a much earlier chapter, I told you about SMART goals and about the difference between a goal and an outcome. It's time now to be bold and courageous and to put your own outcomes into motion. You are now both the master architect and the master builder of your life.

The Master Builder

I work with clients sometimes who are extremely powerful in their negative, half-empty place. They are willing to withstand incredible pain just for the comfort of staying stuck. They follow a rigid formula of hard work combined with a tough attitude, and they endure this existence over great lengths of time. When they are confronted with "new you" psychology, they go, "Okay, I get it. I see how I have sabotaged myself over and over again."

But *then*, instead of changing their future, they snatch defeat from the jaws of victory by creating a destructive new outcome.

You are going to do the opposite. You have your blueprint; you also know *how* to build a reality. You now have all the tools you need to complete your ultimate masterpiece. So, get to work!

If your outcome is to run, you are not to going to merely "run more." Your blueprint now says, "I am a gifted, powerful runner. I LOVE RUNNING! Every day that I can get out, I do. I have completely left behind an old identity that I wasn't an athlete. Every day that I get outdoors or on the treadmill, I feel rippling muscles and lactic acid burning my way to a great future. I can't wait until my 10K in six weeks. I love the fact that my mom wasn't a runner, and that she tried to protect me, but now, I AM A RUNNER! I live in my potential now!"

If this is your new story and meaning, can you see how *everything* will shift?

Your action plan is going to say "This week, I am going to run two miles this afternoon. This Tuesday, I am going to run six miles. Wednesday, I am going to have the most incredible rest, and I'm going to read a biography of a great runner. Thursday, I am going to do my twelve miles, and I am going to time myself. Then, I am going to buy some great running shoes. I am going to be focused on my run; I am going to have my weather gear ready. My runs are going to be on my calendar, and I am going to tell people about it. I am going to clear my time because running is an exhilarating part of my life!"

The "greatest version of you" has picked all these incredible actions around the things that are important to you. But, you are also going to have to physically schedule them and put them on your calendar in order to make them real. You need to prioritize your actions and determine the best way to actually fit all of the details into your life.

And, from time to time, you are going to need to go back and re-evaluate your plan. What's working? What isn't? What do you need to tweak to get back on track? *Always, always* do this only as the "greatest version of you."

Do you follow?

From the inside out, you have now designed a Taj Mahal life experience.

The Inevitable You® is in the house and in action.

You've rewired the things that used to hold you back into successes and strengths. You're on fire, you're in this magical place, and now you can authentically *feel good* about the fact that you ARE a Level 10, amazing, powerful, magical, and extraordinary being.

Do you see what's possible now?

- Look at every area of your life (Health, Relationships, Career, Finances, etc.). In each, what are your "greatest version of you" SMART outcomes for tomorrow?

- For the next week?

- For the next month?

- For the next year?

- What is your plan to turn your ultimate "greatest version of you" vision into reality?

- <u>And</u>, what are the actions tied to the plan? Are these actions written down, and are they scheduled on your calendar with the necessary time to complete them?

CHAPTER TWENTY-ONE:
You Are Free

*Welcome to your magical, legendary,
and <u>inevitable</u> life.*

I said that reality was not fixed and that *you* control it. You own it. It's never the storm that creates your reality—you do. Do you concur?

I predicted that there would be fear attached to buying into this. Are you ready for what is going to happen in your life? Do you know which direction will you head from here?

I emphasized that <u>ALL</u> results begin with one thought? Have I effectively made that case?

I explained that emotions catalyze the power of that one thought, and I told you, "You are not broken. There is nothing wrong with you. Your strategies and recipes may have problems, but there is *nothing* wrong with you." Do you get that?

It is *never* a matter of resources; it's your beliefs about what is possible that's important. That's why most lottery winners lose their prize—they don't have programs needed to support wealth, prosperity, and abundance.

But, you do.

Even in the face of a storm, *you are always fine*. You are always in a great place...

There are always three psychological maps in potential play. Are you now aware of how to identify each one and consciously choose which psychology to use and function?

Do you feel your "new fear?" Can you feel it as the new adrenaline of life?

And for those "old you" fears, when they crop up, just honor their intention to protect you, thank them for their desire to guard you, and "deflect" them out the back door to play in the back yard with all your other old fears, old anxieties, and old family of origin programs that you no longer want or need. Tell them to have a good time! If they run back around and knock on the front door trying to come in, just repeat the process. You *will* succeed in banishing them, especially in a higher evolved psychology.

The Inevitable You® is now in action, and I can't wait to see what you create. Good luck and congratulations.

You are free.

EPILOGUE

I have devoted my life to leadership, the study of people, and finding better ways to serve them. You see, I find most people powerful yet oblivious to their power despite their best intentions. I view them as just waiting to return to that magic state of a four-year-old, if they only knew how to do it, with the appropriate wisdom and experience of their current life and age. This book begins to lay out that road map.

The greatest bulk of my client work lies with this crucial question: What most stops us from changing?

While each person has his or her own unique answer to this, we can lump them into a number of general categories:

- We believe that <u>we</u> can't change. We believe that change is possible. We believe that others can change, but we don't believe that we can. We then create a story to hide this truth.

- We don't want to change. Our current condition serves us in a way that we value more or fear less than the changed state. We then create a story to hide this truth.

- We tell ourselves that we don't know how to change. This is a story that we create to hide the truth.

- And sometimes, we simply don't use the tools for change that we know.

Now this last reason, for me, is a cop out in my declaration to serve you. *Mission first, mission always.*

So if you finish this book and still have questions and are still unsure as to how to make that "new you" or "greatest version of you" leap, here's what I ask you. I have worked hard to give you the general toolbox and understanding of why this works. I have presented the buttress to the most prevalent reasons you have that might not allow the use of these tools for change and transformation. I have also given you a detailed section on the power of questions, and finding that one Inevitable® Question that is defying your attempts to accelerate forward.

So here's my recommendation—I have another product based on this book entitled the same, *The Inevitable You®: Live Life By Design Audio Coaching System.* It is over ten hours of audio content that greatly expands upon this book, and the most important piece is a 225-page workbook that is *nothing but questions!* I designed it with as much incredible consciousness that I could muster to allow anyone to go into deep conscious detail of what their old life was, and to capture the excitement and adrenaline of their new life with all the neural design blue print details tailored to *each reader.*

I encourage you to visit my web site: www.theinevitableyou.com for more details and contact information to learn more about how this blue print process will work for you.

Until we meet again, I send you great love and great energy—*you are inevitable!*

12384392R00105

Made in the USA
Charleston, SC
01 May 2012